SURVEILLANCE COUNTERMEASURES

A Serious Guide to Detecting, Evading, and Eluding Threats to Personal Privacy

ACM IV SECURITY SERVICES

PALADIN PRESS
BOULDER, COLORADO

Also by ACM IV Security Services:

Secrets of Surveillance: A Professional's Guide to Tailing Subjects by Vehicle, Foot, Airplane, and Public Transportation

Surveillance Countermeasures:
A Serious Guide to Detecting, Evading, and Eluding Threats to Personal Security
by ACM IV Security Services

Copyright © 1994 by ACM IV Security Services

ISBN 0-87364-763-7
Printed in the United States of America

Published by Paladin Press, a division of
Paladin Enterprises, Inc.
Gunbarrel Tech Center
7077 Winchester Circle
Boulder, Colorado 80301 USA
+1.303.443.7250

Direct inquiries and/or orders to the above address.

PALADIN, PALADIN PRESS, and the "horse head" design
are trademarks belonging to Paladin Enterprises and
registered in the United States Patent and Trademark Office.

Visit our Web site at www.paladin-press.com

CONTENTS

CHAPTER 1

INTRODUCTION TO SURVEILLANCE COUNTER- MEASURES

The privilege of personal privacy is by no means an inalienable right. In today's information age there are any number of agencies actively collecting information on average citizens for various reasons. This information is shared among compatible computer data bases, providing easy access to anyone with the resources to gain entry. Compound this ease of access with the volume of data collected by federal agencies, law enforcement agencies, and credit reporting services, and the amount of information available on any individual is alarming. This gives an adversary with a computer terminal, a telephone modem, and a basic knowledge of information systems the capability to develop a relatively concise picture of anyone's personal life.

For virtually everyone, forfeiting a degree of privacy is the price of living in the modern world. This is acceptable if the information is used for constructive purposes. In many cases, however, interest in people's private lives does not end there. Just a glimpse into the case files of any federal investigative, local law enforcement, or private investigative agency provides unique insight into the degree to which millions of people's private lives are being researched, scrutinized, and even exploited. Although most of the aforementioned organizations' activities are both legitimate and necessary, there are any number of others that collect information on individuals for malicious purposes.

At the most basic level, even unsophisticated criminals will "case" potential targets to develop information that will maximize their probability of success in committing a crime. Criminal organizations will use more sophisticated methods to develop information on individuals they intend to intimidate, exploit, or terminate. Terrorists depend upon thorough targeting information because of the extreme security concerns of their operational methods and the requirement for precise and successful attacks.

Methods of international espionage have become much more aggressive toward nonmilitary interests. With the demise of the Communist threat, the intelligence services of foreign countries, both friend and foe, are competing in a Cold War based on economics. With less emphasis on military advantage and more on economic strength, the number of individuals who are vulnerable to espionage due to business affiliations is vastly increased. Compound this with the ever-increasing practice of industrial espionage conducted between competing businesses, and it becomes clear that the threat to the business sector is truly significant. Another disturbing revelation in this area is the increased frequency with which employers use methods of surveillance to monitor the performance of their employees.

This synopsis of the threat to individual privacy is only a small-scale sketch of the reality. The fact is that any individual who wants to develop information regarding another need only dedicate the time necessary to access the many sources available or commission the services of a private investigative agency to this end. However, many adversaries will not be satisfied with this and will therefore be required to actively develop information. Surveillance is the most commonly employed method of doing so. In fact, investigative agencies rely significantly on surveillance—as do any individuals or organizations that attempt to develop information that is not otherwise available.

This threat to personal privacy and security can only be countered through active measures; that is, surveillance countermeasures. These can be categorized as either surveillance detection or antisurveillance. The former is employed to detect the presence of possible or suspected surveillance, while antisurveillance is used to elude a possible or suspected surveillance. Both methods are further categorized into distinct disciplines.

If a surveillance effort is to be countered, a keen knowledge of surveillance principles and tactics is essential; one must understand how an individual or team of surveillants operates in order to detect or elude the effort effectively. This book addresses principles formed from time-proven methods of countering the most sophisticated surveillance tactics.

Surveillance can be either physical or technical.

Physical surveillance requires the direct involvement of the human element, which simply means that it must involve physical observation of the target by an individual or a team of surveillants. For this reason, physical surveillance assumes a degree of exposure of the effort to the individual under surveillance. Surveillance countermeasures are employed to maximize this exposure—or to force the surveillants to terminate contact in order to avoid it.

Technical surveillance uses equipment such as remotely monitored video cameras, listening devices or "bugs," telephone monitors or "taps," and motion-monitoring beaconing devices to observe, monitor, or record the target's activities. Technical surveillance devices are vulnerable to both physical inspection and technical detection. Again, understanding technical surveillance capabilities is essential to negating their effectiveness or detecting their presence.

Surveillance may be conducted to achieve any number of objectives. Its traditional purpose is to observe or record an individual doing something he would otherwise take measures to conceal. In the context of law enforcement, surveillance is employed to observe a suspect conducting illegal activity. From the private investigative standpoint, the objective might be to observe an unfaithful spouse in the act of adultery. As with these two scenarios, virtually all surveillance efforts are conducted at times when the target assumes a degree of privacy that allows him to act without discretion.

Although law enforcement and national security agencies generally conduct surveillance to achieve objectives that are appropriate and necessary, others do so for various less constructive purposes. Terrorists and assassins rely extensively on surveillance to develop data on their prospective targets. They use it to identify when and where an individual is vulnerable to a lethal attack, just as military reconnaissance patrols develop targeting intelligence for combat forces. The increasing phenomenon of victim stalking is an example of how obsessed or disturbed individuals conduct surveillance against innocents for sinister purposes.

Another objective of surveillance is to develop exploitable information. This encompasses and far transcends mere illegal activities. It is based on the premise that personal information that an individual wishes to keep private can be used against him as leverage through the threat of disclosure. Espionage agencies have long used this practice to blackmail people into spying against their own countries. Those confronted with exploitable evidence developed through surveillance may be coerced to cooperate rather than risk having the information disclosed to their families, employers, or the public. The most common examples of exploitable information are closet homosexuality or vices such as alcoholism, drug abuse, or gambling; but the possibilities are limitless.

No one is immune to the threat of surveillance. This book provides a systematic approach to gaining the expertise necessary to maintain personal privacy and security in the face of this ever-present threat. While the tactics addressed herein have been directed against the most sophisticated surveillance methods employed in the world today, individuals can readily apply these state-of-the-art concepts to their specific concerns.

Although this book presents a wealth of surveillance countermeasures, the actual number of such tactics is unlimited, so the reader should not become consumed with specific tactical examples. The primary value of this book is in the detailed explanation of principles that provide a unique insight into the application of surveillance countermeasures to individual, situation-specific requirements. Again, developing a keen conceptual understanding of how to defeat a surveillance effort is vital to the effectiveness of surveillance countermeasures.

CHAPTER 2

SURVEILLANCE COUNTERMEASURES OVERVIEW

This book provides a comprehensive explanation of surveillance countermeasures principles and tactics based on the developmental detailing of the concepts and their applications. Many of the issues discussed in this overview will be addressed in detail in subsequent chapters. But it is necessary to begin with a basic understanding of how the individual principles and tactics built upon in this book apply to the overall surveillance countermeasures effort.

TERMINOLOGY

The premise of surveillance countermeasures is that an individual is constantly vulnerable to the threat of surveillance. In fact, such countermeasures are the means by which someone who is under surveillance minimizes or negates the specific threat. All surveillance operations will have a primary target or focus about whom their purpose is to develop information. Throughout this book, the target of the surveillance will be referred to as the *Principal*. (In this context it will always be capitalized to distinguish it from other uses of the word.) The vehicle in which the Principal is traveling, either as the driver or a passenger, will be referred to as the *Principal vehicle* (although when the tactics being addressed are centered around a vehicular surveillance, the vehicle may also be referred to as simply the Principal for brevity).

The activities of the Principal that he would normally take measures to protect when the threat of surveillance exists are referred to as *protected activities*. These are commonly associated with illegal endeavors, but based on the wide range of surveillance objectives, any Principal has information or conducts activities which he would not want disclosed to potential adversaries. *Protected information* is any that provides insight into protected activities.

Surveillance Principals generally fall into into three categories: soft, hard, and overt.

The *soft* target is one who, based on his status and background, is not expected to suspect surveillance coverage. This assumes that he has had no training in countermeasures and is not likely to employ them as a standard practice. A soft target is not involved in any illegal or clandestine activity and, therefore, should have no reason to suspect surveillance coverage.

The *hard* target is one who can be expected to be surveillance-conscious, based upon his status and background. A hard target represents a more sophisticated challenge to a surveillance team because he is expected to have had formal countermeasures training and might employ them during his travels as standard practice. Common examples of hard targets are espionage agents and terrorist operatives, both of which are thoroughly trained in surveillance countermeasures tactics and employ them constantly in order to survive. Reading this book will qualify the Principal as a hard target. In most cases, such a target's training will consist of countermeasures tactics that can be employed in a natural, inconspicuous manner. This is important to the sophisticated target, because if a surveillance team observes him employing countermeasures, it will assume he is dirty and intensify the efforts against him. Regardless of training, any target who is engaged in illegal or clandestine activity will be considered hard.

An *overt* target is one who, based solely on his present status, is expected to be surveillance-conscious and employ countermeasures as standard practice. The overt target represents the greatest challenge to the surveillance team because he can be expected to be more aggressive or overt in his actions. The most common example of an overt target is an espionage agent operating under official diplomatic status out of official missions or embassies. Such targets constantly assume that surveillance coverage is present and will conduct a thorough ritual of surveillance detection and antisurveillance maneuvers prior to conducting any operational activity. Other examples of overt targets are suspected flight risks who are out of jail on bond or people being escorted by protective services personnel.

As this book addresses surveillance tactics that are employed in a total surveillance team effort, the effort will be referred to as a *surveillance team* throughout. An optimally effective surveillance team will normally consist of 12 individuals and six vehicles. This may increase in some cases and be unnecessary in others; even single-person surveillances are not uncommon under certain circumstances. A surveillance team and all of its encompassing capabilities will be referred to in some contexts as a *surveillance effort*.

A surveillance team consists of surveillants traveling by foot, vehicle, or a combination of both. Throughout this book, a vehicle the surveillance team uses in an operation will be referred to as a *surveillance vehicle*. Individual team members will be referred to as *surveillance operators*, or simply *operators*. They will be further identified as *foot operators* when engaged specifically in foot surveillance. Any resource available to the surveillance team will be referred to as a *surveillance asset*, a term that can apply generically to a surveillance vehicle or operator but that will also include other capabilities, such as a technical device or an observation post.

When a surveillance operator observes the Principal, he is said to have *command* of him. In a vehicular surveillance operation, the vehicle in command of the Principal is referred to as the *command vehicle*. A foot operator in command of the Principal is referred to as the *command operator*.

Surveillance Principals come in all shapes, sizes, and sexes. A well-rounded surveillance team will consist of a good mix of male and female operators. Throughout this book, however, the Principal and surveillance operators will be referred to in the masculine for brevity.

DEFINITIONS AND PRINCIPLES

Surveillance countermeasures are actions a Principal takes to identify or evade a surveillance effort. They are based on known surveillance principles and tactics. Surveillance countermeasures consist of surveillance detection and antisurveillance, both of which are further specialized based on their method of application and the form of surveillance they are intended to defeat.

Surveillance detection consists of the Principal's efforts to identify the presence of surveillance. It is conducted by one of four methods, or any combination thereof: passive detection, active detection, countersurveillance, and technical surveillance detection. The first three are employed against physical surveillance threats, while the latter is directed against the wide range of technical surveillance threats.

Passive surveillance detection is nothing more than the Principal's observation of his surroundings. He will simply watch for activities of surrounding vehicles and pedestrians that are suspicious and possibly indicative of surveillance. Passive detection requires an understanding of surveillance principles and tactics, which can be used to evaluate observations.

Active surveillance detection involves specific, usually preplanned maneuvers the Principal makes to elicit conspicuous reactions from a surveillance effort. By executing a surveillance detection maneuver, the Principal attempts to force members of the surveillance team to react in a manner that allows him to isolate and identify surveillance.

Countersurveillance is the use of people other than the Principal to detect the presence of surveillance. With countersurveillance coverage, the Principal does not have to observe his surroundings to identify the presence of surveillance, as is the case with active and passive surveillance detection. Countersurveillance coverage will normally be established around a preplanned surveillance detection route that the Principal will travel. The route will incorporate certain maneuvers or take advantage of terrain and physical structures that enable the countersurveillance to isolate and identify the surveillance coverage.

Technical surveillance detection consists of methods directed against the technical surveillance threat. This is a very broad category due to the many types of technical capabilities a surveillance effort can employ. It can be accomplished either through a physical search or a technical search using electronic countermeasures equipment. Most commonly, technical detection uses devices such as frequency scanners or spectrum analyzers to detect radio transmissions or technical monitoring devices that may be indicative of surveillance coverage.

Antisurveillance consists of actions the Principal takes to evade an identified or suspected surveillance. For the purposes of this book, antisurveillance is distinguished as either physical or technical. Physical antisurveillance measures are used to evade the efforts of a surveillance team that is following the Principal physically. Technical antisurveillance measures are used to deny or neutralize the effectiveness of a technical surveillance capability.

Surveillance countermeasures, whether surveillance detection or antisurveillance, can be conducted either overtly or covertly. With *overt surveillance countermeasures*, the only objective is to detect or elude surveillance, with little regard for the fact that the surveillance effort will know that the Principal is practicing countermeasures tactics. Overt countermeasures are characteristic of overt targets. One example is when an individual runs a red traffic light in order to elude a possible surveillance. Any surveillance effort observing this action would become highly suspicious that the individual is practicing antisurveillance.

Covert surveillance countermeasures attempt to detect or elude a surveillance effort in a manner that would give the surveillance effort, if present, little or no indication that the Principal is, in fact, practicing countermeasures. Throughout this book the terms covert and discreet will be used interchangeably.

A *denied* area or location is one to which the Principal has open access but the surveillance team does not. Denied areas consist primarily of residences or establishments in which the Principal has freedom of movement but to which the surveillance team's entrance is restricted for practical purposes. This restricted access does not preclude a surveillance team from entering surreptitiously.

A *target area* or location is one that is the focus of a *technical attack*. A technical attack is a technical surveillance operation directed against a target area.

CHAPTER 3

SURVEILLANCE PRINCIPLES AND TACTICS

Surveillance countermeasures are conducted under the assumption that surveillance is always possible. They are based directly on the tactics of surveillance they are used to detect or defeat, and thus a keen understanding of the opposition's tactics is essential to their effective execution. This chapter will detail how the surveillance threat operates. It is by no means a comprehensive tutorial on surveillance; rather, it is designed as an overview to be used as the basis for understanding the countermeasures principles and tactics addressed in subsequent chapters.

PHYSICAL SURVEILLANCE

Physical surveillance is the systematic, discreet observation of an individual to develop information regarding his activities. It differs from technical surveillance in that the surveillance operators must observe the Principal physically. It is the only means by which a Principal can be observed constantly over an extended period of time.

A professional and effective surveillance is orchestrated in a systematic manner. This is accomplished through tactics that will ensure discreet coverage of a Principal. A surveillance operation can only be effective if it goes undetected by the Principal or anyone else, such as neighbors, associates, employees, passersby, and so on.

Surveillance is employed to identify

and document significant activities of a Principal that satisfy the objectives of the specific operation. Developing information through surveillance is a progressive and often lengthy process. It is from many pieces of information that an overall picture of the Principal's behavioral patterns is developed.

A surveillance operation will normally begin with limited information regarding the Principal's activities. It may begin by developing such information in order to identify those times or activities on which to focus the surveillance effort. As information is developed, *target pattern analysis* is conducted to determine which patterns the surveillance team can exploit to anticipate the Principal's actions more effectively. This also enables the surveillance team to determine which times and activities may be significant in satisfying the objectives of the operation, as opposed to those that are routine and insignificant, allowing it to cover a Principal efficiently by concentrating on those with the highest potential payoff. It also serves to limit the amount of time that surveillance operators and vehicles may be exposed to the Principal.

A surveillance vehicle or operator can use anything that offers *concealment* to obstruct the Principal's view. A surveillance vehicle provides a degree of concealment, as do structures such as buildings. Another example of concealment might be the positioning of a surveillance operator inside a building so as to observe the Principal out of the windows.

Darkness is another form of concealment.

Cover and *cover for action* are concepts that are extremely critical to the effectiveness and security of any surveillance operation. *Cover* is a broad term that generally applies to anything a surveillance operator or vehicle uses to appear natural when observation by the Principal, countersurveillance, or any other third parties is possible. During a foot surveillance operation, cover consists primarily of pedestrians in the area. During a vehicular surveillance operation, cover consists primarily of vehicular traffic on the roads. In both situations, the surrounding traffic enables the surveillance operator or vehicle to blend in and appear as any other pedestrian or vehicle.

Cover for action is a more specific term that refers to actions the surveillance operator takes to establish a plausible reason for being in a given location or undertaking a given activity. For example, a surveillance operator can use a telephone booth for cover, but he must actually place money in the phone and make a call to establish a cover for action. More specific applications of cover and cover for action will be addressed throughout this book, including the manner in which they support surveillance countermeasures.

There are two primary types of physical surveillance: fixed and mobile.

Fixed surveillance consists of observing the Principal's activities at a specified location from a static position. Such operations will only satisfy specific objectives because they provide limited insight into the Principal's overall activities. They are normally employed when it is suspected that the Principal will conduct protected activities at a specific location, such as his residence, his workplace, an associate's residence, or an establishment he frequents. Fixed positions are normally manned by surveillance operators or monitored through remote video equipment. A surveillance team may use any number of fixed positions during a fixed surveillance operation. One common example of a fixed surveillance is when the surveillance team establishes static positions along a designated route to confirm the Principal's direction of travel. Most fixed surveillance operations use an established observation post that enables surveillance operators to maintain constant, discreet observation of the specified location.

Mobile surveillance is employed to satisfy any objectives of physical surveillance that cannot be accomplished through a fixed operation. In mobile surveillance operations, the surveillance team observes the Principal's activities while he is traveling. Of course, this requires that surveillance operators and vehicles move with him. Mobile surveillance operations are conducted either on foot, by vehicle, or with a combination of both. Mobile and fixed surveillance may be used concurrently to enhance the effectiveness of an operation. Fixed observation posts are frequently employed to support mobile surveillance operations.

Phases of a Mobile Surveillance Operation

A mobile surveillance operation is a fluid sequence of tactical maneuvers that are dictated primarily by the actions of the Principal. (This is not to say that the Principal has any advantage against a professional surveillance effort.) In order to effectively cover the Principal, the team must maintain synchronization through a phased operation with a unity of tactical discipline and purpose.

A comprehensive surveillance operation is conducted in four phases: the stakeout, the pick-up, the follow, and the box. It will progress through these phases based on the Principal's actions. Ideally, an operation will move through these four phases and then shift the order in which they are implemented in reaction to the Principal's activities.

The *stakeout* involves positioning surveillance vehicles or operators based on how the team intends to establish initial command of the Principal. This consists of the logical coverage of a specified area to ensure that when the Principal appears, the team will be able make a smooth and effective transition from static positions to a mobile surveillance follow. This is accomplished primarily by the use of a *boxing method* intended to cover all routes of travel into and out of the specified area.

The *pick-up* occurs when the surveillance team establishes initial command of the Principal. It is the result of a successful stakeout or surveillance box. The *follow* begins immediately after the pick-up. This phase encompasses all aspects of the surveillance operation that occur while the Principal is under command.

The *box phase* begins as the Principal stops during a surveillance follow. As with the stakeout box, a standard surveillance box is a logical positioning of surveillance vehicles or operators to cover all routes of travel out of a specified area. The primary difference between the two types of boxes is that with the standard surveillance box, there is a degree of command over the Principal because the surveillance team is certain he is positioned somewhere within the box.

Methods of Mobile Surveillance

There are four primary methods of mobile physical surveillance: vehicular surveillance, foot surveillance, combined foot and vehicular surveillance, and progressive surveillance. The first three are purely mobile surveillance; progressive surveillance makes use of mobile surveillance, fixed surveillance, or a combination of the two.

Vehicular Surveillance

Vehicular surveillance operations are conducted to determine the Principal's activities while traveling by vehicle. They are normally used to determine general travel patterns rather than to develop specific information. Vehicular surveillance is effective when employed at the outset of an operation to collect data for target pattern analysis while minimizing the initial exposure of operators to the Principal.

Vehicular surveillance is an integral aspect of most physical surveillance operations. The Principal will rarely travel exclusively by foot. Even when operating against a Principal who travels primarily by public transportation, the surveillance team must rely on vehicles for control and mobility. Although the surveillance team will rarely observe a Principal conducting protected activity while traveling by vehicle, it is understood that the Principal will travel by vehicle to reach the location where such activity may occur.

Vehicular and foot surveillance share many operational tactics. Vehicular surveillance, however, is a more exact science because routes of travel are generally restricted to, or channelized by, established roadways. This can be used to the advantage of a capable surveillance team, but in the same way, it can be used to the advantage of a resourceful Principal. There is also less maneuverability in vehicular surveillance because a surveillance vehicle has less flexibility to turn around and reposition discreetly. This disadvantage is overcome only by expertise in teamwork and tactical applications.

A vehicular surveillance will begin with the stakeout of a specified location at which the surveillance team expects to establish initial command of the Principal. The location is selected based on assumptions about when and where the Principal is likely to appear. Primary stakeout locations are the Principal's residence and workplace. The Principal is normally expected to stay the night at his residence, depart sometime during the day, and return to his residence by the end of the day. He can also be expected to appear at his place of work with some degree of regularity. These standard patterns provide the surveillants with locations that promise a high probability of establishing command of the Principal.

The tactics normally used for staking out an area to pick up the Principal for a mobile surveillance follow are referred to as boxing. A stakeout is basically a logical positioning of surveillance vehicles to attain initial command of a Principal as he either travels through a specified area or emerges from it. The stakeout box consists of positioning surveillance vehicles in such a manner as to control routes of travel out of a specified area. These vehicles are positioned for pick-up as the principle drives out of the stakeout box along any of the possible routes of travel.

The surveillance team may use an observation post to observe a specific location in support of its stakeout. Observation posts are normally positioned to observe a residence, business, or workplace. Using an observation post saves the team from having to expose a vehicle in order to observe the location. A surveillance team may also employ a mobile observation post, normally a van that can be parked within line of sight of the target location for observation.

The pick-up phase of the surveillance begins when the Principal is first observed and ends when the follow phase begins. The follow phase begins after the Principal exits the stakeout box and the surveillance vehicle along his route of travel maneuvers to assume command of him for the mobile surveillance follow. The follow phase encompasses all surveillance activities conducted while the Principal is mobile. During the follow, the surveillance team must have at least one vehicle (the command vehicle) with visual observation of the Principal, normally following from behind.

The following distance of the vehicular surveillance team will be dictated primarily by the terrain, available cover, traffic obstacles, and traffic hazards. Cover will normally consist of surrounding traffic into which the team can blend to appear natural. Traffic obstacles such as dense traffic, traffic signals, and construction zones may deter the surveillance team from maintaining command of the Principal. Therefore, the team will normally need to maintain a closer following distance when confronted by significant traffic obstacles. Traffic hazards such as highway interchanges offer the Principal high-speed or multiple avenues of escape. Since it is important that the surveillants have command of the Principal when entering a traffic hazard, they will normally close their following distance when approaching one.

A tactically sound surveillance team will exchange command vehicle positions frequently during the course of the follow to remain discreet and minimize the exposure of any one vehicle. This may be done at any time but primarily in reaction to a turn by the Principal. Exposure can also be minimized by utilizing the cover and concealment of surrounding traffic.

Communications equipment is critical to the vehicular surveillance team. The ability of all of the surveillance vehicles to communicate allows them to rely on the transmissions of the command vehicle to guide their activities. This enables team members to maneuver effectively without having to rely on their visual observations of the Principal or other surveillance vehicles. A surveillance vehicle normally has two operators, a driver and a navigator. The navigator reads a map and directs the driver. When in the command vehicle position, the navigator transmits the Principal's location and actions to the entire team. Otherwise, the navigator will monitor the radio in order to track the Principal's location on the map and direct the driver to maneuver in a manner that supports the operation.

The mobile surveillance follow will transition directly to the box phase anytime the Principal stops, excluding normal traffic stops. This consists of the surveillance team maneuvering to box positions around the Principal's stopping point. As with the stakeout box, surveillance vehicles will establish positions along each of the Principal's possible routes of departure in order to pick him up when he begins to move and leaves the box location. The surveillance team will normally position a vehicle in a location from which its occupants can physically observe the stationary Principal vehicle and inform the team when it begins to move. As the Principal begins to move, the pick-up phase is again initiated. The follow phase begins again after the Principal exits the box and the surveillance vehicle along his route of travel maneuvers to assume command of him for the mobile surveillance follow.

Night surveillance operations are significantly different from those conducted in daytime. The basic tactics remain the same, but darkness imposes many additional considerations. The very nature of night surveillance dictates that the surveillance team must concentrate on more technically intricate concepts and tactical applications. This may include the use of night vision equipment or specialized controls to prevent the surveillance vehicle's brake lights from projecting when the brake pedal is engaged. Since the surveillance vehicle's lights are the most visible signature the team will project to the Principal, the lights must be in proper working order and must not project in an unusual manner that may bring the vehicle to the Principal's attention.

Due to the darkness, it is difficult for the Principal to recognize a surveillance vehicle by any means other than the lights. This is an advantage in itself, but there are many disadvantages inherent in this aspect of night surveillance as well. These are directly related to the fact that there is generally less traffic cover at night. In crowded urban areas, the lights of surrounding vehicles can make the surveillance team virtually invisible to the Principal. As the hour gets later and the traffic density decreases, the surveillance vehicle's lights make it virtually impossible for it to remain discreet. In the absence of sufficient cover, vehicle lights are detectable at a significant distance, making it easier for the Principal to detect surveillance vehicles.

Foot Surveillance

Foot surveillance operations are conducted to determine the Principal's activities while traveling by foot. Such operations normally have limited objectives. Foot surveillance is most effective when there is specific information to indicate that the Principal will conduct significant activities in an anticipated area while on the ground. This allows the team to concentrate its operators on the ground rather than dividing assets evenly between foot and vehicular surveillance when it anticipates that the Principal's travels will be restricted to foot movement.

The mobile foot follow employs most of the same tactics as vehicular surveillance and consists of the same four phases of a surveillance operation. A primary difference from vehicular surveillance is that foot operators have much more flexibility to maneuver quickly in any direction. This is a significant advantage in the stakeout phase because foot operators are not constrained by having to position themselves to pick up the Principal traveling in only one direction.

One disadvantage of the foot stakeout is the degree of cover and concealment available. Whereas operators manning a surveillance vehicle parked along the road have some physical concealment, a foot operator standing alongside the road runs a greater risk of exposure. For this reason, foot operators in the stakeout box will attempt to maximize available cover and devise a plausible reason for being where they are. They will also attempt to position themselves in locations that provide physical concealment from the Principal, such as inside a building looking out of the window.

Foot surveillance operators will normally follow and observe the Principal from behind. They will be positioned to follow directly behind him, behind and on the opposite side of the road, or a combination of both. Following distance will be dictated by terrain, amount of cover, and traffic obstacles. Cover in foot surveillance consists primarily of pedestrian traffic into which the surveillance operators can blend, but it may also include plausible activities that they can undertake.

Cover and concealment are normally more important considerations in foot surveillance because foot operators tend to be more vulnerable to unexpected maneuvers by the Principal. Foot operators must assess the surrounding terrain constantly for cover and concealment opportunities in the event of a turn, stop, or reversal of direction by the Principal. It requires a high degree of skill and discipline to react naturally to such unexpected moves by the Principal and transition to an effective cover or concealment position without drawing his attention.

For the foot operator, traffic obstacles consist primarily of traffic or pedestrian density and busy roadways that are difficult to cross quickly. As with vehicular surveillance, significant traffic obstacles will normally dictate that the foot surveillance team close its following distance.

Communications equipment is an important aspect of effective foot surveillance, just as in vehicular surveillance. Concealed communications equipment enables each foot operator to transmit and receive information regarding the Principal's observed activities. Surveillance operators can communicate silently in the Principal's presence by depressing the microphone button to produce static in response to another operator's questions.

Since body communications equipment is expensive, it is not common to all foot surveillance teams. Teams that operate without it must rely on visual signals to communicate. This dictates that each foot surveillance operator either maintain visual observation of the Principal or another signaling operator in order to continue in the follow. Therefore, a team without body communications equipment must follow much more closely, which invariably results in a higher degree of exposure to the Principal for all of its operators.

Foot surveillance at night provides the surveillance team with an enhanced degree of concealment. The darkness is of great benefit to the foot surveillance operator, but it can also be of great benefit to a Principal who is attempting to elude surveillance. The advantages gained by increased concealment with the darkness can be easily negated by limited visibility. Surveillance operators can maximize the advantage of darkness by employing night vision equipment. Because there are fewer pedestrians at night, surveillance operators are not as concerned with appearing suspicious to surrounding pedestrians and can therefore operate more freely. A team without body communications equipment at night is at a loss because it is difficult to rely on visual signals in darkness.

Public locations (i.e., areas or establishments that offer open access to the public) pose unique considerations to the foot surveillance team. They differ from public streets because they normally have physical or notional boundaries and a greater concentration of people. These two factors impose unique restrictions on foot surveillance operators. In most cases, public locations will force the operators much closer to the Principal than they would otherwise allow themselves to become.

The number of public locations to which the Principal may lead the surveillance team is unlimited, including restaurants, stores, malls, parks, and airports. Public locations offer varying degrees of cover, which is critical due to the confined operating area. A surveillance team is particularly vulnerable to exposure in public locations because there is a higher probability of unexpected maneuvers by the Principal.

Public locations are also unique in that they may have varying levels of terrain. These are normally separated by channelized avenues of travel such as stairways, escalators, or elevators, which again may leave operators vulnerable to exposure. One other disadvantage the surveillance team will encounter in public locations is multiple entrances and exits, which allow the Principal to enter and exit at any time by a number of avenues. This may require the team to commit more surveillance operators to the public location in order to maintain team integrity. The result may be the exposure of multiple surveillance operators to the Principal, even when the team has body communications equipment.

Combined Foot and Vehicular Surveillance

Combined foot and vehicular surveillance operations employ all mobile surveillance disciplines comprehensively. Such operations are conducted to observe all of the Principal's activities during a specified period. They require that the entire team possess a high degree of tactical and technical expertise to ensure an effective transition between vehicular and foot surveillance. Obviously, such operations increase the exposure of operators and vehicles to the Principal. Long-term operations will normally require that both be replaced throughout to maintain security.

Combined foot and vehicular surveillance integrates the individual tactics of both modes. The most unique aspect of this method of surveillance is that as the Principal transitions from vehicle to foot or vice versa, the surveillance team must also do so while simultaneously maintaining command of the Principal and avoiding exposure. It is during these periods of transition that the team will experience the greatest difficulty maintaining command due to the sudden shift in the operation.

As the Principal stops his vehicle and transitions to ground, the surveillance vehicles will attempt to drop off foot surveillance operators in positions that will maximize their probability of successfully continuing the follow. The team must realize that dropping multiple operators in the same location or in the vicinity of the Principal vehicle represents an unacceptable risk of exposure. The navigators will therefore analyze the area's terrain by examining the map to determine the best location for foot operators to be dropped to integrate into the follow.

As this transition is made, the tactics of foot surveillance predominate the operation. Surveillance vehicles will support the foot surveillance in progress. One will be dedicated to establishing a static position to observe the Principal vehicle. This is critical in that if the surveillance team loses command of the Principal on the ground, the surveillance vehicle observing the Principal will at least be able to inform the team if he returns. The other surveillance vehicles will support the foot operators on the ground. If they are equipped with body communications gear, this will consist of relaying their radio transmissions as well as reading the map and providing directions. Surveillance vehicles can also transport foot operators throughout the operational area in support of the foot surveillance.

When foot operators are receiving adequate support from surveillance vehicles, any remaining vehicles will establish box positions to pick up the Principal vehicle when the transition back to vehicular surveillance occurs. As the Principal travels back to his vehicle, all of the surveillance vehicles will prepare to switch to the vehicular follow by picking up foot operators and maneuvering to boxing positions around the Principal vehicle's location. As the Principal enters his vehicle and travels away, the surveillance team will execute a pick-up and follow similar to that of the box phase of the mobile surveillance operation.

Progressive Surveillance

Progressive surveillance is the phased coverage of a Principal to determine specific travel patterns or specific routes of travel. It is conducted through the use of mobile surveillance, fixed surveillance, or a combination of the two. Progressive operations can only satisfy the very limited objective of determining the route or routes of travel that a Principal takes from a common point of origin. They are normally used when limited resources such as personnel or communications equipment restrict the surveillance team from conducting extended foot, vehicular, or combined operations. Progressive operations are also used when security is the highest priority. They are the most secure method of surveillance because the team's degree of exposure to the Principal is limited.

Progressive surveillance is applicable to any surveillance team under various circumstances. The most notorious practitioners of progressive surveillance are terrorists and assassins, because such coverage allows them to determine a specific travel pattern of a potential victim securely and identify a point along that route which is suitable for an attack.

If the objective is to determine the route that the Principal takes to work, the operation will begin at his residence. If the objective is to determine where he goes after work, the operation will begin at his workplace. The objective may be further narrowed to determining the Principal's route of travel only on specific days when protected activity is expected to occur.

The basic concept of the progressive surveillance is to follow the Principal or observe his travel from a point of origin. The Principal is observed as he travels from the point of origin until he reaches a particular location, where the surveillance is terminated. The next phase of the operation is based from the location where the previous one was terminated. At this point the Principal is observed as he travels farther along the route to another location, at which point the operation is again terminated. The next phase begins at the last termination point, and the process is repeated until the operational objective is satisfied.

A concept that is common to both mobile and fixed progressive surveillance operations is the use of decision points. These are locations that provide the Principal with the option to turn or continue straight. The most common example is a street intersection. Each phase of the progressive surveillance operation will normally be centered on determining the Principal's direction of travel from the decision point at which the surveillance will be terminated. The next phase will then be centered on determining his direction of travel from a decision point along the route of travel based on the origin of the previous phase's terminating decision point.

Public Transportation

The surveillance of a taxicab is basically the same as standard vehicular surveillance. The surveillance team will note the specific cab number and any company logos on the taxi the Principal enters. This information may assist the team in identifying the location to which the Principal was driven in the event that command is lost. This requires that the team contact the taxicab company and attempt to elicit the information. If surveillance vehicles are not available, using a second taxicab to follow the Principal's is virtually the only option. This tactic is extremely risky because most cab drivers will be alerted to a following taxi.

The surveillance of city buses involves a completely unique surveillance concept. Due to the generally slow movement and frequent stopping of most buses, a surveillance team will attempt to position itself ahead of the Principal's bus route because it is virtually impossible to maintain a vehicular follow from the rear. The surveillance team will match the bus number to city route maps to determine destinations and stop locations. The team will attempt to place a surveillance operator on the bus with the Principal but will avoid doing so at the stop where the Principal boards. An operator will board at a stop further along the route or, if there is time, at one prior to the Principal's. The vehicular surveillance team will then position itself at stops along the route before the scheduled arrival of the bus in anticipation of the Principal's eventual exit.

Surveillance on mass transit systems such as subways or metros is the most difficult kind. Even when surveillance operators have body communications equipment, they will be unable to communicate from the station to the team outside. Such a communications link is only possible by telephone or through an operator moving aboveground to relay information. Even when the foot team inside the station is able to inform them which train the Principal enters, the vehicular team outside must attempt to deduce which stops along the route may be the Principal's destination. Multiple train exchanges will virtually destroy team integrity. For this reason, the foot surveillance team will attempt to place as many operators on the train with the Principal as possible, entering with him and exiting behind him, to maintain integrity and a surveillance capability at his destination.

Surveillance on trains and planes is basically the same. The team will attempt to determine the Principal's destination as early as possible. In lieu of any other means, it will do so by listening as the Principal purchases his ticket. Obviously, this tactic places a surveillance operator in close proximity to the Principal.

If the Principal is flying and his flight plans were not previously disclosed, it will be virtually impossible to have a vehicular surveillance capability at his destination unless another surveillance element can be contacted for support. Under such circumstances, if the team intends to continue the follow at the destination, it must place as many operators on the plane as possible.

For train travel, the route may be one which allows the surveillance team to send vehicles to the destination to either meet or catch up to the foot team. Again, the team will attempt to place as many operators on the train as possible.

At the destination of either a train or plane, if the team has transported communications equipment, operators can rent vehicles for a limited vehicular surveillance capability.

TECHNICAL SURVEILLANCE

Technical surveillance is the use of technical electronic equipment to monitor or record the activities of the Principal. Activities can be monitored by video, audio, or motion detection. Activities are primarily recorded by means of video or audio tape, but techniques such as intercepting facsimile transmissions or down-loading computer data banks may also be used.

A surveillance effort may employ technical surveillance either to supplement an ongoing physical surveillance operation or as the sole means of monitoring the Principal's activities. Just as the term implies, technical surveillance requires the knowledge of technical electronic concepts. An understanding of these technical concepts is equally important in detecting the presence of technical surveillance.

Audio Surveillance Techniques

Audio surveillance is the most widely used means of technical surveillance. It consists primarily of placing audio surveillance devices in the target area to provide an audio product to a monitoring surveillance element. Although there are less intrusive ways to conduct audio surveillance, access to the target area is generally assumed.

One method that does not require access uses a light system

that transmits a laser beam modulated by audible sounds into the target area. Such a system requires a line of sight, ideal weather conditions, and a reflective surface in the target area to direct the light back to a specialized receiver for signal demodulation. This system is most effective when the reflective surface is inside the target area, but a window on the perimeter can also be used. Microwave signals are also used to capture and transmit audio impulses through a reflective beam, although this method differs from laser transmissions in that microwave beams can penetrate physical barriers other than glass. Another method that does not require physical access to the target area uses a directional microphone or parabolic dish. As all of these techniques require line of sight, they are relatively ineffective against structurally contained target areas and so are employed primarily in open terrain.

An audio surveillance device consists of a microphone to receive and convert audio energy into electrical energy. The device must have a means of transmitting the signal to a receiver that reconverts the electrical energy into audio energy. The means of transmission will be radio frequency, wire, or a combination of the two.

System power is a primary consideration in the use of audio devices. Those with an organic power source will serve only a limited purpose or require repeated access to the target area for servicing. Audio devices can be wired to the electrical system of the target area for uninterrupted power, but there are disadvantages to this technique, which will be addressed in this and later chapters. A device may also receive power through a wire from a remote source, but this method too has drawbacks, which will be addressed.

Radio Frequency Transmission

Radio frequency (RF)-transmitted audio devices consist of a microphone coupled with a transmitter. Such a device will transmit the audio signal to a remote listening post. The listening post must be located within the transmission range of the device, and the degradation to transmission range resulting from structural, atmospheric, and electromagnetic interference must be factored in. RF-transmitted devices will normally contain a power source, but some are configured and installed to operate from the target area's electrical system. Battery-operated devices have a significant advantage in that they can be installed quickly and with relative ease, minimizing the time the installer needs to spend inside the target area. Battery-powered devices can be introduced into the target area through less intrusive means, such having an unwitting Principal carry one in.

For any battery-operated listening device, RF can be used to activate and deactivate the power source for extended use. Specialized, energy-conserving circuitry is another option for extended battery life. One primary disadvantage to RF listening devices is that the signals transmitted are highly susceptible to detection by spectrum analyzers or interception by frequency scanners. This is another advantage to a RF deactivation capability—it can be used to decrease this vulnerability.

Wire Transmission

A wire transmission device is a microphone wired directly to the monitoring activity. The restrictions imposed by a wire connection may or may not be disadvantageous, depending on the location of the monitoring activity and the ease with which the wire can be concealed or disguised. For instance, if the monitoring activity is in an adjacent hotel room, then a wire will not be a significant detractor. A wire installation will generally produce a better-quality audio output, although the quality of the signal will decrease as the wire is extended. Another advantage of a wire device is that power can be supplied through the wire to the microphone, negating the problem of limited battery life. Despite the advantages of wire transmission devices, RF-transmitted audio devices are generally preferred because if a wire device is discovered it will lead directly to the monitoring activity. The installation of a wire device is also more difficult and time-consuming.

Combined RF and Wire Transmission

A combination RF and wire system consists of a microphone wired from the target area to a transmitter, which is outside the target area but still closer than a listening post could otherwise be positioned. The remote transmitter sends the audio signal to the monitoring activity via a RF link. Such a system avoids running a wire directly to the monitoring activity and at the same time overcomes degradation to the signal that may result from the physical structure surrounding the target area. It is also possible to supply power to the device through the wire connection. This allows the device to receive power from a transmitter that is connected to a constant power source, or at least from one that is easier to access for battery servicing than the device located in the target area.

Telephone Monitoring Techniques

Telephone monitoring techniques are generally classified as bugging or tapping. Although bugging a telephone may also involve introducing a RF-transmitted listening device (as described in the previous section) into the telephone unit, this discussion will be limited to modification of the telephone's circuitry to manipulate one of its organic microphones. Telephone tapping is the interception of the electrically generated audio signal from the telephone line originating from the target telephone area.

Telephone Bugging

Telephone bugging is a relatively simple practice, given a basic knowledge of the mechanics of a telephone unit. Bugging requires physical access to the telephone either in the target area or before it is taken in. A telephone unit has three organic microphones: one in the receiver (earpiece), one in the transmitter (mouthpiece), and a microphonic ringer. Manipulation of the microphonic ringer is rare because it requires the introduction of a separate microphone into the telephone wiring to create an interface. Either the receiver or transmitter microphones can be activated by manipulating the telephone circuitry to monitor all audio activity in the area surrounding the telephone. This makes the telephone an audio surveillance device in the target area, whereas telephone tapping is limited to intercepting conversation that actually takes place over the telephone. Telephone bugging also requires the incorporation of a telephone tap to extract the intercepted audio from the carrier telephone line.

Every telephone is serviced by a telephone company central office, which constantly supplies electrical energy to the telephone through the telephone lines. When the telephone is on the hook, electricity is only routed through its microphonic ringer and directly back to the central office to complete the circuit. When it is taken off the hook by lifting the handset and releasing the hook switch, the electrical circuit is opened through the entire telephone system to activate the receiving and transmitting mechanisms.

The process of telephone bugging is based on manipulating the telephone in order to produce an off-the-hook status at all times. This is done by bypassing hook switch contacts to generate a constant flow of electricity through the entire telephone unit. Depending on the method of manipulation, this in effect makes the receiver or transmitter an active listening device. This can be done by a number of methods using the telephone's internal wiring or installing independent bypass circuitry. Depending on the method used and the microphone targeted, the bugging process may require the installment of a resister to regulate the current flow or a capacitor to enhance the quality of the audio.

Telephone Tapping

Telephone bugging as discussed in the previous section requires that the telephone line originating from the targeted telephone be tapped. Telephone tapping refers to extracting the electrical signal generated by the target telephone and converting it to audio energy to be monitored. Since telephone bugging requires access to the target telephone, it is usually difficult if not impossible. Even when the target telephone is not bugged for audio intercept in the target area, telephone tapping can still provide the surveillance effort valuable information by intercepting all telephone conversations over the tapped line. Telephone tapping is also used to intercept facsimile transmissions and computer interface traffic over the targeted telephone line.

Telephone taps can be administered anywhere along a telephone line between the target telephone and the telephone exchange. Taps are normally placed as close to the target telephone as possible because the farther away the more difficult the process. Inductive couplers can be placed on the line to extract the audio signal, or intercept wiring can be attached to the telephone line physically. Inductive couplers can be monitored via either a wire connection or a RF-transmitted signal. Although wire taps can be placed anywhere along the line, they are normally employed at transfer points, such as a junction box, because the intercepted signal is clearer at these points and no splicing or crimping is necessary—leaving no indication of the tap after the operation is complete. A telephone line intercept configuration may include the attachment of a telephone decoder to identify the telephone numbers associated with each outgoing call.

Another form of telephone monitoring not necessarily associated with tapping is the intercept of cordless and cellular telephone transmissions. Cordless telephones are the least secure means for telephone conversations because they can be intercepted by a standard frequency scanner. Cellular telephones normally require additional expertise and equipment for intercept, but they are nonetheless vulnerable.

Technical Physical Monitoring

Technical physical monitoring is the use of technical equipment to monitor the activities of the Principal. This primarily consists of monitoring the Principal's location to assist the overall surveillance effort. The primary method of physical monitoring is the use of tracking devices. Tracking devices generate a signal which can be monitored from a receiver in a standoff position. The tracking system will inform the surveillance effort of when the Principal is moving, his direction of travel, and his distance from the receiver. Since the tracking device must be collocated with the Principal in one way or another, the most common application is to place it on the Principal vehicle. Rarely will the surveillance team have an opportunity to place the tracking device directly on the Principal, but another possibility is to place it in a personal belonging that the Principal frequently carries, such as a briefcase.

Another method of physical monitoring is thermal imaging. This is the use of passive infrared equipment that detects and amplifies electromagnetic energy emitted as radiated heat and converts it into a visible form. Thermal imaging is used primarily for tactical surveillance applications to scan large areas and detect the radiated heat of people and machinery. Specialized thermal imaging equipment can also be used to monitor the movement of a Principal inside a denied structure such as a building or house.

Automation Systems Technical Surveillance

Personal and office computers are becoming increasingly lucrative sources of information regarding an individual's personal activities. An office computer is not normally associated with personal or private information, but much of the information on an individual's office computer, such as an activity calendar or a data base of associates, would prove most valuable in support of a surveillance effort. Certainly, the information on a personal home computer would support a comprehensive surveillance effort. In many cases, the information contained in a computer's data bank may provide the information that satisfies the overall objective of a surveillance operation.

A computer that is used as a stand-alone and is not connected to any other is referred to as a personal computer. A computer that is connected to another computer or network is referred to as an automation system. Many people network their personal home computers to a system via a telephone modem. A computer in any configuration is vulnerable to technical surveillance.

Automation systems are most vulnerable to technical surveillance because any computer in the system can be accessed by any other computer in the system. Additionally, the lines of communication, normally telephone lines, that connect the network can be penetrated at any point to gain access to the system. A surveillance team may gain access to a target computer through an unprotected computer in the system. With some technical expertise, a surveillance team can penetrate the system's transmission lines and determine the access codes necessary to enter the target computer through either technical analysis or trial and error.

The surveillance team may use a manipulative programming process referred to as "malicious software" to facilitate the surveillance effort. This consists of a computer programming code that is hidden within another computer software program. Most commonly, malicious software takes the form of computer viruses that reproduce onto other programs in the computer. Viruses, however, normally serve a destructive purpose such as erasing data files and so are not consistent with the objectives of surveillance. The most effective use of malicious software for surveillance purposes is the introduction of a "Trojan horse program" onto the target computer's software. A Trojan horse program is one that is concealed within another otherwise useful computer program. The most common application of a Trojan horse is on the computer's disk operating system because this is the program commonly booted each time the computer is used. The most effective use of a Trojan horse for surveillance purposes is to program in a "trap door." By gaining one-time access to the target computer, a surveillance team can introduce a Trojan horse with a trapdoor, which will then allow it to gain future access by invoking the trapdoor command.

With some additional programming expertise, the surveillance team can transfer the Trojan horse into the target computer through the computer network. This involves the use of another malicious software technique, referred to as a "network worm."

Personal computers are much less vulnerable to technical surveillance since there is no network to be used for access. Virtually the only way for a surveillance team to access all computer data is to gain physical access to the computer by employing surreptitious entry techniques into its location, which will normally be the Principal's residence or workplace. The only technical methods involved at this point are those necessary to defeat the computer's access control measures if present.

A surveillance team can receive information from a target computer that is in use through the exploitation of compromising emanations. Computers radiate electromagnetic pulses from the screen and other components when in use. By using technical equipment that isolates the frequency of the target computer's radiations, a surveillance team can in effect read the computer monitor from a remote location.

CHAPTER 4

OBSERVATION

Observation is a critical aspect of surveillance detection. It also supports antisurveillance, particularly in identifying the need to elude surveillance by detecting it. The Principal's perceptive ability to observe and retain specifics regarding the surrounding environment enables him to identify indications of surveillance and subsequently confirm them through repeated observations of surveillance operators or vehicles.

A sophisticated surveillance team rarely commits tactical errors that allow the Principal to identify its presence during an isolated incident. Although there are specific surveillance detection maneuvers that are designed to expose surveillance immediately, most depend on the Principal's ability to observe his surroundings and confirm any suspicions such observation might elicit at subsequent times and locations.

OBSERVATION PRINCIPLES

Observation is the act of seeing or fixing the mind upon something for the purpose of recognizing and retaining some fact or occurrence. It is conducted through the body's senses of perception. Perception is an individual's awareness of the elements of environment, gained through physical sensation in reaction to sensory stimulus. Sensory stimulus is perceived by the body's senses, which consist of sight, hearing, touch, smell, and taste. For surveillance detection purposes, observation relies primarily on the sense of sight, but it can be enhanced by hearing and, to a much lesser degree, smell.

Effective observation requires a conscious and continuous effort. This consists of a keen awareness of surrounding activity to observe and retain the images of specific individuals, objects, and occurrences. This includes the perception of shape, size, and features; colors, shades, and lighting; and speed, time, and distance. The process of observation consists of three sub-processes: attention, perception, and retention. Attention is the aspect of observation that is most critical to surveillance detection, because without attention, perception and retention are impossible. Attention is the awareness of surroundings that provide the sensory stimulus on which perception is based. People will normally apply voluntary attention to the activity they are undertaking. An item or occurrence that does not fit within an individual's frame of reference for what is the status quo normally draws involuntary attention. For example, someone may walk through a crowd of faceless people until a person with a limp immediately draws his involuntary attention. People who are particularly large or small have this same effect, as do bright colors and loud or sharp sounds.

As mentioned, an individual's attention is normally focused on the activity he is undertaking at the time. His attention is limited to items and occurrences that have direct impact on that activity, unless it is seized by an unusually large, loud, or relatively unanticipated item or occurrence. An individual driving down the road will normally focus his attention on those factors which impact that activity—primarily the traffic and road ahead. The Principal practicing surveillance detection, on the other hand, must expand his attention to include the entire surroundings.

The skill of observation requires a knowledge of the principles of perception and an understanding of how they are employed. The most basic detractor one must overcome in attempting to enhance perceptive skills is the tendency to perceive and retain only those items or occurrences that fall within his range of interests or understanding. Everyone has a unique range of interests and understanding based on mental capacity, education, and background.

Personal interests are conditioned throughout a lifetime, and to expand observation beyond those requires a conscious and focused effort. Perception is also limited by an individual's base of knowledge. The mind tends to either subconsciously filter out items and occurrences for which there is no frame of reference by which to describe them in known terms or retain them for subsequent retrieval. An individual must be constantly aware of these tendencies in order to overcome their impact on observation.

Every individual perceives his surroundings uniquely. In the context of observation for the purposes of surveillance detection, the Principal's frame of reference for how people and vehicles are observed must be expanded through concentration and training. The unassuming individual may view all individuals equally—or ignore them equally. A person who holds ethnic prejudices will immediately avert his attention to those who do not conform to his standard of "normal," whereas those who do conform will pass unnoticed. A person who has been the victim of a violent crime at the hands of an someone of a particular race or category of persons will display vigilance in directing his attention to those who meet this profile in comparison to others individuals around him. Another common example of how attention is programmed is that attractive individuals of the opposite sex will normally seize people's attention. This brief psychological synopsis illustrates the impact an individual's frame of reference has on his attention.

As mentioned previously, perception and retention are only possible after attention is applied. Most people's perception of what a surveillance operator looks like comes from Hollywood interpretations and spy novels. This frame of reference will only serve to filter out the actual surveillance operators because, contrary to popular perceptions, they will be among the most unassuming individuals on the streets. This perception must be overcome for surveillance detection purposes because otherwise the Principal's attention will be focused on misconceived indicators.

OBSERVATION AND SURVEILLANCE DETECTION

A basic understanding of the principles of observation is a critical aspect of surveillance detection. Much of surveillance detection depends on observing possible or suspected surveillance operators or vehicles, retaining their images or key aspects thereof, and confirming that they are surveillance operators or vehicles through subsequent observation. Once again, perception and retention are contingent on attention. The Principal's voluntary attention must transcend the frame of reference that has developed over his lifetime and he must apply attention to all surrounding activity to the greatest degree possible. Then, through a keen knowledge of surveillance tactics and an ability to detect indicators of surveillance, he can eliminate those individuals and vehicles that are not indicative or suspicious and key on those that are.

Any sophisticated surveillance effort operates based on a keen understanding of the principles of observation. A surveillance effort will conform to what most people see as the status quo or norm with respect to the surrounding environment. This minimizes or negates the degree to which it draws the involuntary attention of the Principal. Although the Principal cannot discount unique individuals and vehicles immediately, it is safe to say that they will rarely be representative of a sophisticated surveillance effort because of the attention they attract.

For the purposes of surveillance detection, the primary objective of observation of surrounding individuals is to retain their characteristics—consisting of features, form, dress, and mannerisms—for later recognition. It is not feasible to retain all of these for each individual observed. The Principal must attempt to key on those characteristics that are the most dominant and difficult to alter. By so doing, he can concentrate on retaining specific characteristics of a number of surrounding individuals in a short period of time. By keying in on characteristics that are difficult to alter, the Principal does not squander mental resources retaining those that are easily altered and possibly of no subsequent value.

Observation of Features

Body features consist primarily of face, head, and hair. Three things that directly impact these are gender, race, and age, though these are not considered features in and of themselves because none can stand alone as an identifying characteristic for surveillance detection purposes.

Body features are the most accurate characteristics by which to identify individuals. With the exception of hair, these are generally the most difficult and time-consuming to alter. Body features, however, are the most difficult to observe because they require that the Principal be close to the individual under scrutiny. The tactically sound surveillance operator will rarely place himself in a position that allows this degree of observation. Additionally, for reasons which will be detailed in later chapters, there are some long-term tactical disadvantages to the Principal's being in close proximity to a surveillance operator.

Facial features consist primarily of the eyebrows, eyes, nose, mouth, lips, chin, and ears. They can also include wrinkles, scars, dimples, birthmarks, moles, complexion, or other such markings as applicable. With many individuals, these variables can be the most distinguishable for observation purposes. Generally, however, the primary features will be the ones used for retention. The most effective method of observing an individual's facial features for retention is to first develop an overall image of the face and then key on the most distinguishable feature or features.

The head is normally distinguished by its shape. Although this could also qualify as a characteristic of form, it is included in the category of body features because of its impact on facial features and the overall development of a facial image. Additionally, the shape of the head includes the shape of the face. The shape of the head is generally differentiated as being round, high in the crown, bulging at the back, flat at the back, or keel (egg)-shaped. The shape of the face is distinguished by its height and breadth. Although oval is the most prominent facial shape, faces can also be round, square, broad, fat, thin, or long. Body fat, or the lack thereof, may have a significant impact on the shape of a face.

Hair is a significant aspect of an individual's appearance. It can be a very deceiving feature, however, when one is operating against a sophisticated surveillance effort. As will be discussed in a subsequent section, hair is the surveillance operator's quickest and most effective method of altering his appearance without resorting to elaborate disguise techniques. Hair is generally distinguished by color, length, texture, body, and style. The lack of head hair is a particularly prevalent feature. Facial hair, which is primarily distinguished by color, texture, and style, is yet another prevalent feature. Additionally, body hair such as arm and leg hair can assist detection observation.

The observation of surrounding vehicles for surveillance detection purposes also depends on the perception of features. Whereas each individual's appearance is unique in many ways, there is much more duplication among vehicles with regard to makes, models, and colors. For this reason, the ability to observe features that may distinguish one vehicle from like models is critical to surveillance detection. Unique features such as dents, scratches, tires, hubcaps, designs, and distinguishable license plates are examples of those the Principal must concentrate on in order to isolate a possible surveillance vehicle from others on the road. At night, features such as a unique headlight appearance are useful for surveillance detection.

Observation of Form

Form consists of shape, build, and size. The overall body shape is formed by the neck, shoulders, trunk, stomach, buttocks, hips, legs, feet, arms, and hands. Distinguishable aspects of any portion of the body can be isolated for observation purposes. Body shape is directly affected by body fat and muscularity. The fit of clothing must be considered, as it may distort perception in the observation of body shape. Build is generally categorized as heavy, stocky, medium, slender, and thin. This too is directly affected by body fat and muscularity and can also be distorted by clothing. Size is a relative characteristic based on individual perceptions. It is generally described in terms of height, width, and breadth. In assessing an individual's size, one must factor in the distortion to perception caused by distance.

Height is categorized as short, medium, and tall, but it should be estimated specifically by feet and inches. In assessing an individual's height, the observer must factor in the distortion to perception that may occur when he and the individual under observation are situated at different levels. Additionally, height can be altered by thick soles or heels on the shoes. Body width and breadth are particularly subjective and relative to the perception of the individual making the observation. For example, some individuals may be heavy or stocky in build but relatively small in overall size, whereas others are simply big without necessarily being fat or muscular. Again, width and breadth can be distorted by clothing. Finally, posture can have a significant effect on overall form, but this is normally considered a characteristic of mannerisms.

Form is also applicable to the detection of surveillance vehicles. From a distance, a vehicle's form is more readily distinguishable than its features. At night, the form projected by the silhouettes of following vehicles is one of the few things which can be discerned for surveillance detection purposes. This same silhouette characteristic also applies to forms inside a vehicle, such as those of the occupants.

Observation of Mannerisms

Mannerisms are those characteristics or idiosyncrasies that are unique to an individual. They are peculiarities in action or bearing, including posture, stride, pace of motion, and voice quality. The number of examples is unlimited. Mannerisms that stand out or appear awkward can be effectively exploited for surveillance detection.

An individual's demeanor and bearing are established through myriad mannerisms. These are actions which are either programmed over a lifetime or result from physical characteristics. Those that develop through the years become subconscious actions and therefore can only be controlled by a conscious effort. Mannerisms that result from physical characteristics are much more difficult to alter because the mind cannot control and conceal what the body is unable to. For these reasons, the observation of unique mannerisms in surrounding individuals is an important aspect of surveillance detection. Whereas a surveillance operator can effectively alter appearance through disguise, most mannerisms require a continuous conscious effort to conceal or alter, and many are physically impossible to conceal.

Physical mannerisms such as stride and posture are the easiest to observe. Unique physical mannerisms such as limps and nervous twitches are particularly conducive to surveillance detection. In addition to representing themselves through physical mannerisms, people do so through their outward manner or demeanor. Demeanor generally consists of attitude, disposition, and temperament. These factors significantly influence how people carry themselves. For example, extroverted individuals normally display a more outgoing, positive, or aggressive demeanor.

Regardless of his degree of extroversion or introversion, every individual exudes unique characteristics of demeanor that require a conscious effort to alter or conceal.

Some of the most difficult mannerisms to control are those associated with nervousness and anticipation. Although surveillance operators will attempt to maintain an inconspicuous demeanor at all times, there is a natural tendency to become driven by the increase in adrenaline brought about by a surveillance operation. This can result in conspicuous actions or mannerisms such as pacing, focused staring, and continuously checking the watch.

Other mannerisms that are unique to surveillance operators and may be exploited in surveillance detection observation are those associated with wearing body communications equipment. Many sophisticated surveillance teams equip surveillance operators with concealed body communications equipment for enhanced operational effectiveness. As a result, operators develop such tell-tale ideosyncrasies as adjusting upper-body equipment, talking into their chests, fidgeting with their hands in their pockets, and checking their ears with a finger.

Observation of Dress

Habits of dress are characteristics an individual develops over a lifetime. They are influenced by factors such as background, heritage, status, profession, and life-style. Some individuals are meticulous in the selection and maintenance of their clothing while others give this aspect of their outward appearance little concern. A person's position along this spectrum of dress dictates the fashion in which he feels natural, comfortable, and confident.

This is an important factor from the perspective of surveillance detection because individuals have a tendency to appear unnatural when dressing in a manner that does not conform to their standard of fashion. A surveillance operator may be required to dress in a manner that is not natural for him in order to blend in with a particular situation and surrounding. The appearance of dress and mannerisms associated with discomfort or unfamiliarity may be detected by the Principal.

Dress is an aspect of appearance that is more readily observed from a distance than many others, such as body features. Unless someone is making an active effort to observe the dress of surrounding individuals, his attention will normally be drawn only to clothing that does not conform to his standards. Unique, striking, or colorful clothing will usually draw involuntary attention. Although clothing is an important criterion for the observation of surrounding individuals for detection purposes, a sophisticated surveillance team will make efforts to minimize the impact that dress might have on the compromise of surveillance operators. They will therefore dress in a manner that conforms to the standards of the surrounding populace. Furthermore, the surveillance effort will likely capitalize on the ease with which appearance can be altered by changing clothing in order to degrade the effectiveness of surveillance detection.

Dress also includes jewelry. A sophisticated surveillance effort will generally forego wearing it because the purpose of jewelry is to attract attention—which, of course, the surveillance effort is actively attempting to avoid. There are, however, some cases in which wearing jewelry lends itself to surveillance detection. Most basically, there are some minor items of jewelry, such as wedding bands and watches, that surveillance operators may continue to wear despite the risk. A watch is an extremely important piece of equipment to surveillance operators. Since they will rarely own enough watches to match the number of times they are required to change clothing, they will generally accept the risk of wearing the same watch. Rings will generally leave identifiable marks such as tan lines on the fingers. When a surveillance operator changes clothing, he may opt to continue wearing a ring if there is no replacement, because otherwise the resulting identifiable mark will appear even more conspicuous to the individual practicing surveillance detection.

Observation of Disguise

The fact that a sophisticated surveillance effort will use disguise to minimize the probability of detection is an aspect of surveillance detection that can make observation difficult. The initial exposure of a surveillance operator to the Principal is not critical, but all subsequent instances of exposure disproportionately increase the probability of detection. The use of disguise allows a surveillance team to project the appearance of different individuals, making it much more difficult for the Principal to isolate a single surveillance operator for detection.

Recall that for the purposes of surveillance detection, observation involves concentrating on features, form, dress, and mannerisms. Surveillance operators use disguise to alter each of these aspects of appearance and thereby deceive the Principal. Many characteristics of appearance are easy to alter, while others are difficult if not impossible. Most features require extensive disguising techniques to conceal or alter. The primary exception to this is hair, which is the single most effective means of altering appearance. By cutting, dying, or restyling hair, or shaving facial hair, a surveillance operator can drastically alter his appearance.

Form is altered primarily by clothing. Changing to or from loose-fitting clothing can project the illusion of a different form. Deceptive devices such as shoulder pads or pregnancy pillows may also be used to alter form. Height can only be altered by thick-soled or heeled shoes, which are readily detectable through observation. Changing posture can also alter form. Surveillance operators use clothing to alter appearance by simply changing clothing from one portion of a surveillance operation to another. Altering mannerisms is more difficult because it requires constant concentration on the part of a surveillance operator. Some mannerisms are physically impossible to alter or conceal.

Although disguise makes surveillance detection much more difficult, there are techniques that can be used to minimize its effectiveness. The first critical factor to understand is that if a disguise is not complete, it actually increases the surveillance operator's vulnerability to detection by an actively observant Principal. Normally the degree of disguise that a surveillance operator employs is proportionate to the degree to which he has been exposed to the Principal. This is a subjective judgment that is also influenced by an assessment of how observant the Principal may be. In many cases the surveillance operator will employ only a partial disguise as a standard security precaution after a period of minimal exposure to the Principal. A total disguise is reserved for circumstances in which the surveillance operator was forced relatively close to, or received a degree of scrutiny from, the Principal.

This can be exploited in surveillance detection. The Principal should practice observation in a manner that is natural and unalarming. This serves to deceive surveillance operators into employing partial disguise as opposed to total disguise. One of the most effective methods of surveillance detection is to confirm that a surveillance operator is using disguise. By using a partial disguise, a surveillance operator may alter some characteristics of appearance while leaving others unaltered. For example, the surveillance operator may shave his mustache, restyle his hair, and change clothes, but leave on the same pair of shoes, the same watch, and walk with the same stride. This can completely reverse the effects of disguise by confirming to the observant Principal that surveillance is present.

Observation at Night

Observation is significantly limited at night due the obvious physiological limitations of the eyes. Visual illusions are also common when observing at night. An understanding of the principles of darkness adaptation will assist in the effectiveness of night observation.

Darkness adaptation is the process by which the human eye increases in sensitivity to low levels of light. Since vision is made possible by reflected light, effective observation is directly proportional to the degree of light available. Although individuals vary in degrees and rates of dark adaptation, eye sensitivity generally increases about 10,000 times during the first 30 minutes in the dark. After that point eye sensitivity increases very little. Visual sharpness at night is about one-seventh of what it is during the day, significantly reducing visual acuity. This dictates that object identification at night is generally limited to silhouettes and forms. Depth and color perception are also affected. At night, color perception is generally limited to distinguishing between light and dark colors, and even this is dependent on the intensity of reflected light.

Adaptation is adversely affected by exposure to bright lights such as matches and headlights. In order to maintain darkness adaptation, the eyes should be covered to avoid the effects of such lights. Recall that initial adaptation takes up to 30 minutes. Recovery from exposure to bright lights can take up to 45 minutes. Adaptation to darkness is adversely affected by the use of night vision devices. If full adaptation is made before using night vision devices, however, it can be regained within two minutes after their use. The use of night vision devices decreases the senses of hearing and smell due to the concentration required for effective sight.

There are two methods of observation that can be used to enhance visual effectiveness in darkness. Both are based on the fact that central viewing, or looking directly at an object, is ineffective at night due to the night blind spot that exists during low illumination. At night, it is essential to avoid looking directly at a faintly visible object because of this night blind spot.

Scanning is a method which enables the Principal to overcome many of the physiological limitations of the eyes as well as reducing confusing visual illusions in darkness. This method consists of scanning from left to right, or right to left, using a slow, standardized eye movement. **Figure 1** depicts two typical scan-

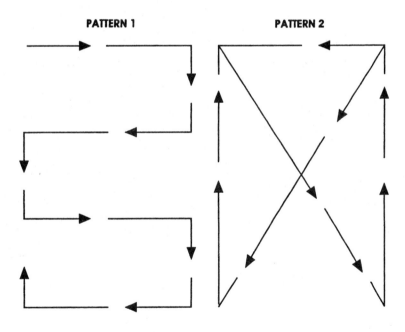

FIGURE 1
Two typical scanning patterns.

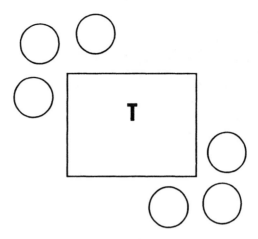

FIGURE 2

Points of observation around the target object for use in off-center viewing.

ning patterns. Off-center viewing is another way to avoid the limitations of central viewing at night. This technique consists of viewing an object by looking slightly above, below, or to either side rather than directly at it. **Figure** 2 depicts points of observation (circles) around the target object.

Even when off-center viewing is used, the image of an object becomes a solid, bleached-out tone when viewed for longer than three to five seconds. For this reason, it is important to shift the eyes regularly from one off-center point to another to maintain an uninterrupted peripheral field of vision.

CHAPTER 5

PASSIVE PHYSICAL SURVEILLANCE DETECTION

Passive physical surveillance detection is conducted during the course of the Principal's standard activities, when no unusual action is being taken. Recall that the very nature of physical surveillance dictates that the surveillance team risks a degree of exposure to the Principal. This possibility of exposure exists regardless of the Principal's actions.

Passive physical surveillance detection makes maximum use of enhanced observation practices (covered in the previous chapter) to defeat the principles and tactics employed by a physical surveillance team addressed in Chapter 3. Anyone concerned with personal security should practice passive detection routinely as a standard, baseline security measure, even when there is no specific reason to suspect surveillance.

Initially, the Principal should proceed as though every vehicle and individual on the streets are surveillance assets. By employing passive detection, the Principal will develop indications of surveillance if it exists. At that point, the Principal may choose to employ active surveillance detection measures or antisurveillance measures against the identified or suspected surveillance effort. As one becomes more experienced in surveillance detection, it becomes easy to initially identify suspicious individuals or vehicles and recognize them when observed again.

A keen understanding of surveillance principles and tactics is critical to the effective application of passive physical surveillance detection. A Principal can exploit his knowledge of the tactics a surveillance effort will employ against him for detection purposes. A surveillance team will operate in a logical and systematic manner to maximize coverage and minimize exposure. A sophisticated surveillance team can operate against an unwitting Principal for extended periods without providing any indication of its presence. Against a Principal who is surveillance-conscious, trained in surveillance detection, and aware of physical surveillance practices, however, the surveillance team faces a greater risk of compromise. Against such a hard target, the surveillance effort may opt to use more operators or more sophisticated measures such as technical surveillance equipment to minimize the probability of exposure. Therefore, it is obviously to the Principal's advantage that the surveillance team not suspect he is conducting surveillance detection.

Since the Principal conducts passive physical surveillance detection during the course of his standard activities, he will give no indication to the surveillance team that he is doing so if he employs it properly. This is an important aspect of passive detection, primarily due to a surveillance team's reaction to a Principal it identifies as surveillance-conscious, which was discussed previously.

TARGET PATTERN ANALYSIS

As addressed in Chapter 3, a surveillance team will conduct target pattern analysis to determine which patterns in the Principal's activities it can predict and exploit more effectively. The team will analyze travel routines, specific routes used, dates and times of specific activities, and standard speeds and modes of travel. This enables surveillance operators and vehicles to position themselves in the most effective manner.

The concept of surveillance detection is based on the assumption that the threat of surveillance is always possible. If a Principal does not conduct all activities and employ at least passive surveillance detection based on this assumption, then surveillance will probably remain undetected. Many people with something to protect make the critical mistake of conducting surveillance detection only when they are actually engaged in activities that would be damaging if a surveillance team were to observe them. This will rarely result in the detection of surveillance, primarily because effective surveillance detection is based on the *constant* application of passive detection measures to identify indicators of surveillance. In conducting surveillance detection only at specific times, the Principal will probably take actions that are not consistent with the target pattern analysis the surveillance team has conducted. Such alterations in patterns will serve to confirm to the surveillance team that the Principal does indeed have something to hide—and will probably result in continued and enhanced surveillance coverage.

The Principal should conduct target pattern analysis, just as the surveillance team would, to support the surveillance detection process. The Principal will analyze his own activity patterns to develop a picture of what the surveillance team, if present, has observed. This analysis is based not only on the assumption that surveillance coverage is always possible, but also on the assumption that it has been present for some time, and that the surveillance team has made sufficient observations regarding the Principal's activities to conduct a thorough pattern analysis.

By making a comprehensive evaluation of his own activity patterns, the Principal uses his knowledge of surveillance principles and tactics to develop a concept of how a surveillance team would employ coverage. Again, it is important to note that identifying activities that are vulnerable to surveillance and should be altered is not the purpose of target pattern analysis. Any significant alteration of established activity patterns will only result in enhanced caution on the part of the surveillance effort. The only exception to this rule is when the Principal conducts target pattern analysis to identify activities that make him vulnerable to a suspected or feared terrorist attack or a similar type of violent assault.

The Principal should also incorporate the perceived objectives of the possible surveillance coverage into the analysis process. A surveillance operation is conducted to observe and document activities that satisfy the objectives of the operation. Although the possible objectives of a surveillance operation are unlimited, they may involve developing evidence for legal prosecution or other purposes, identifying protected activity that can be used against the interests of the Principal, or developing information that can be exploited as leverage against the Principal in interrogation or negotiation. Identification of the opposition's possible operational objectives is normally as simple as identifying potential adversaries and the purposes for which they might employ surveillance. Although surveillance detection is a worthwhile practice as a standard security precaution even when no surveillance is suspected, a logically conceived perspective regarding protected information and activities that potential adversaries might seek to observe provides a degree of focus to the effort.

In conducting target pattern analysis, the Principal should consider the threat of fixed surveillance and progress through the four phases of a mobile surveillance operation, applying his knowledge of surveillance principles and tactics to his identified activity patterns. In regard to the threat of fixed surveillance, for example, the Principal will identify specific locations and activities that the team would be likely to use fixed surveillance to observe. He then identifies specific positions that surveillance assets may exploit, thereby becoming aware of locations that warrant special attention while conducting passive surveillance detection.

Pattern analysis is particularly effective when based against the threat of a surveillance stakeout in preparation for a mobile pick-up. By identifying which locations a surveillance team would select to establish a stakeout box, the Principal can determine specific positions the team would man. The primary locations for stakeout consideration are the Principal's residence and workplace. Other possibilities include frequented establishments and the residences of relatives and associates. In evaluating stakeout positions, the Principal should also assess where fixed observation posts or mobile surveillance systems might be located to support the stakeout effort.

A sound understanding of surveillance boxing tactics is essential to identifying where stakeout box positions might be located. By applying such knowledge to the potential stakeout location, the Principal can identify specific locations where a surveillance team would position assets to facilitate a secure and effective mobile pick-up. This assessment enhances the Principal's awareness of where to focus his observation when departing any potential stakeout area. Area knowledge is necessary to analyze possible stakeout locations; when the Principal is not familiar with the area, he should examine a map to determine such locations.

PASSIVE VEHICULAR SURVEILLANCE DETECTION

In the stakeout, the surveillance team will be positioned to pick up the Principal as he passes through or departs the stakeout location. This requires that surveillance operators be positioned to observe for the Principal and pull out as he passes their location. In the vehicular stakeout, box positions will be established primarily by surveillance vehicles, but foot operators may be used to observe locations that cannot be covered securely by a vehicle.

A surveillance team is particularly vulnerable to detection in the stakeout phase because operators must remain in static positions for extended periods of time. Additionally, although the team will have some idea of where the Principal will initially appear, the fact remains that he could appear in a location that leaves the team vulnerable to compromise.

As the Principal leaves an area that he has assessed as a possible location for an opposition surveillance stakeout, he should observe for vehicles or individuals meeting the profile of those employing stakeout tactics. He should be familiar with vehicles that are normally in the area of the possible stakeout and be able to identify those that appear alien and do not blend with others in the area for whatever reason. The Principal should discreetly note the license numbers of any suspicious vehicles when possible.

When he has determined that the stakeout box may be positioned around a denied location such as a residence or workplace, the Principal should observe for indications of a trigger. A trigger is a surveillance vehicle or operator that is positioned to initially observe the Principal as he departs a denied area or enters his vehicle. Since this requires line of sight observation, the trigger will be detectable by the Principal unless there is sufficient cover and concealment. Vehicles with an individual or individuals inside that are parked in a position to observe the Principal should be retained as an indicator of a surveillance stakeout. The Principal can inconspicuously observe for such positions while departing the denied area, walking to his vehicle, while unlocking the vehicle, and when negotiating traffic to pull the vehicle out.

When departing or passing through the possible stakeout area, the Principal will observe for indications of the pick-up. The pick-up requires that a vehicle pull out from a stationary location and follow the Principal. The tactics of surveillance dictate that there are optimum positions for a surveillance vehicle to be situated in order to establish command of the Principal securely and effectively. The most basic positioning for a pick-up is when the surveillance vehicle (S) parallel parks on the right side of the road on which the Principal vehicle (P) may pass (see fig. 3).

Although this position offers a high probability that the surveillance vehicle can pull out and establish command of the Principal successfully, it is vulnerable to detection. The reason for this is that it will give the Principal a good look at the surveillance vehicle—at an angle which may allow him to see that it is manned. Additionally, such a position may cause the surveillance vehicle to appear more suspicious as it pulls out after the Principal passes. Despite the detractors noted, this type pick-up position is widely used, particularly when there is sufficient cover from other vehicles parked on the side of the road and traffic traveling on the road.

The best pick-up positions for surveillance vehicles are those which can be established off the main road of travel. Such positions allow the surveillance vehicle to complete the assignment without being in the Principal's line of sight as he passes by. Parking lots are often suitable locations for pick-up positioning. The most common and readily available locations for pick-up positions are roads that run perpendicular and join the main road of travel. By parallel parking on such roads, the surveillance vehi-

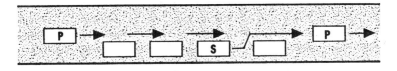

FIGURE 3
Basic positioning used by a surveillance team in order to establish command of the Principal securely and effectively.

cle can observe its designated stakeout location and pull out to establish command of the Principal (see fig. 4).

When selecting a pick-up position in a parking lot or on a perpendicular road, the surveillance vehicle will attempt to ensure that it can make an unimpeded entry onto the main route of travel. The primary obstacle is traffic. To lower the probability that traffic will impede entry, positioning should be based on the Principal's anticipated direction of travel. On two-way roads the pick-up surveillance vehicle should always select a position that allows it to enter the main route of travel from the right side as the traffic flows. This ensures that the surveillance vehicle can make a right turn onto the main to route pick up the Principal. Making a left turn makes it more difficult to enter the main route because the surveillance vehicle is impeded by traffic traveling in both directions. This applies to a lesser degree on one-way roads. Although the probability of traffic from the road to be entered is the same from either side, a surveillance vehicle attempting a left turn onto a one-way road may still be impeded by oncoming traf-

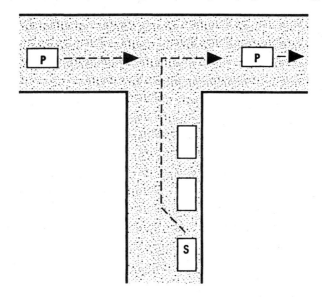

FIGURE 4

A road that is perpendicular to the Principal's main road of travel is a common location for a pick-up position.

fic. These considerations are applied less rigidly in residential or rural areas where traffic is light and presents a negligible obstacle.

Based on his understanding of stakeout pick-up positions, the Principal will observe for indications of their use. There are a number of indicators he should focus on when observing for surveillance vehicles parked parallel on the side of the road (recall that priority should go to vehicles parked on the right side of the road that can pull out quickly to follow).

First, the Principal will observe for parked vehicles that are manned. The standard manning for most surveillance vehicles is a driver and a front seat passenger—most commonly two males. Surveillance operators in a vehicle on stakeout must ensure that they not only appear inconspicuous to the Principal but also to others who may approach them or notify the authorities of suspicious activity. An individual in the passenger seat with the driver's seat vacant should not be discounted because the surveillance team may use this arrangement to appear more natural to the Principal or surrounding populace. Surveillance operators in vehicles may use the seats to block the view of passing traffic, but if they make the tactical error of forgetting to remove their seat belts/shoulder straps, passing traffic can observe them easily even though they may have employed all other principles of discretion.

At night, light from his headlights and other surrounding illumination will assist the Principal in observing silhouetted persons or objects in parked vehicles. Additionally, during the course of a surveillance operation, surveillance vehicles tend to accumulate trash. A poorly disciplined team may leave trash or beverage cups on the dashboard that can be observed by passers-by. Exhaust from a running vehicle is yet another indication that it is manned and ready to maneuver. If the driver has the brake pedal engaged, even when the surveillance vehicle is not running, the brake lights will project.

While surveillance operators are in box positions during periods of inclement weather, such as rain or snow, they have to keep their vehicle windows clear to observe for the Principal. They will do so primarily with windshield wipers and the vehicle defroster. Although this is necessary, it makes surveillance vehicles stand out, as they will be among the only vehicles parked along the road with clear windows that can be seen into. This is particularly true in the case of snowfall, but it also applies to icy conditions and, to a lesser degree, rainfall. The Principal should observe for these indicators when conducting surveillance detection in inclement weather.

As the Principal identifies vehicles that display indicators of surveillance boxing, he will retain their images for subsequent recognition. After passing, he will look back through the side or rearview mirror to see if the vehicle in question pulls out to follow. At night it is often easier for the Principal to see vehicles that pull out to follow because of the sudden appearance of headlights.

It is much more difficult to observe for pick-up vehicles parked in parking lots or on perpendicular roads because of the additional cover this usually affords them. Additionally, it is much more obvious that a Principal is surveillance-conscious when he can be observed visually checking every such location. A vehicle that the Principal observes pulling out and following from these positions offers the primary indicator that a surveillance is being conducted from them. Again, he should pay more attention to vehicles pulling out from the right side of the road.

The primary purpose of passive vehicular surveillance detection is to identify vehicles that might be indicative of surveillance coverage. The ultimate objective of passive vehicular surveillance detection is to identify the same vehicle in two separate locations that are unrelated or incoincidental. Ideally, the Principal will detect indications of surveillance during the pickup, but it is rarely that simple. During the follow phase, the surveillance team is constantly vulnerable to detection because at least one surveillance vehicle must maintain line of sight observation of the Principal. The team must also react discreetly to unanticipated maneuvers by the Principal. Due to these facts alone, passive surveillance detection can be extremely effective, even against a well-disciplined surveillance team.

Recall that with a fully integrated surveillance team, a number of separate surveillance vehicles will observe the Principal at different periods throughout the mobile follow. This dictates that the Principal concentrate not only on one or two probable vehicles, but any number of vehicles. Also recall that a comprehensive surveillance effort does not comprise only one trip or day in the life of the Principal. This dictates that the Principal remember for extended periods any vehicles he observes that fit the profile of a surveillance vehicle. For instance, if the Principal observes a suspected surveillance vehicle and then observes it two weeks later at an unrelated location, he has virtually confirmed that he is under surveillance. This example emphasizes the importance of keen observation and retention skills in surveillance detection.

As already mentioned, a well-disciplined surveillance team will only expose one surveillance vehicle at any given time during the mobile follow. For this reason, the Principal will normally observe only for a single possible surveillance vehicle at any one time. An exception is when he is traveling on terrain that facilitates rear observation over a distance, such as straight highways or rural roads. Also, during the mobile phase of a surveillance operation, a well-disciplined surveillance team will rarely provide the Principal with specific indicators of surveillance unless he takes active measures to induce a conspicuous reaction. Since passive detection involves no active measures by the Principal, detection will generally be limited to multiple sightings of surveillance vehicles, suspicious activity observed when a surveillance vehicle is forced close to the Principal vehicle due to traffic, and perhaps an isolated tactical error by the surveillance team.

One particular aspect of the mobile follow that the Principal may be able to detect through passive observation is mirroring. Mirroring refers to the tendency of a surveillance vehicle to duplicate the Principal's maneuvers. This results from the sometimes even subconscious tendency of a driver to continually place the surveillance vehicle in the optimum position to follow and react to the Principal's maneuvers. Although this is more significant in active surveillance detection, it may also be detectable through passive observation. As the Principal navigates through traffic he will observe for following vehicles that appear to be mirroring his actions.

A passive method of eliciting such an action from a possible following surveillance vehicle is to engage the turn signal well in advance of a turn and observe for any vehicle whose driver attempts to position it to make the same turn. Engaging the turn signal on short notice—or failing to signal at all—is an active measure that rarely serves the purpose of surveillance detection against a well-disciplined surveillance team. The reason is that if the driver of a surveillance vehicle is not in a position to make a turn with the Principal securely, he should simply relinquish command to a vehicle that can do so from a more secure distance.

Also with regard to mirroring, anytime the Principal makes a turn, he should observe to his rear to identify any vehicles that also make the turn. This in itself will rarely confirm that a surveillance effort is underway, but it can facilitate surveillance detection by adding to the Principal's mental data base of vehicles he may observe subsequently, thereby confirming it. The obvious exception to this is when the surveillance element consists of one or a few vehicles, dictating more frequent and less secure turns behind the Principal, leaving it much more vulnerable to detection.

Another indicator of surveillance that the Principal may detect through passive observation is pacing. This is another form of mirroring in which the surveillance vehicle tends to gauge the speed of the Principal and travel at that same speed. In doing so, the surveillance vehicle will maintain a standard following distance that may not be consistent with the surrounding traffic. An undisciplined surveillance vehicle may even provide suspicious indicators such as holding back traffic or making erratic maneuvers to maintain the established pacing distance.

Convoying is an indicator of surveillance which is detectable on roadways that afford the Principal a long look back at following traffic, such as highways and rural roads. Convoying is the tendency for surveillance vehicles to maintain an equal distance between each other. Obviously this tendency is only detectable when the terrain allows the Principal to observe two or more surveillance vehicles. Over a period of time and distance, the Principal may detect surveillance vehicles because they meet the profile of maintaining the convoy effect while other vehicles pass by. Streets with a long downward slope provide optimal terrain for observing for convoying vehicles and other indicators of vehicular surveillance. The characteristics of darkness which facilitate the observation of vehicle lights from a distance also enhance the detection of convoying vehicles on appropriate terrain.

Overall, in conducting passive vehicular surveillance detection the Principal should observe for any activity of surrounding traffic that appears peculiar. Even the best surveillance teams will commit tactical errors—maneuvers that appear suspicious because they do not blend with the surrounding traffic. Surveillance vehicles may tend to close their following distance on the Principal when approaching traffic hazards or obstacles such as highway interchanges or busy intersections in order to maintain command. After the hazard or obstacle the surveillance vehicles will return to a more secure following position.

At times during the follow, surveillance vehicles may lose command of the Principal and be forced to travel at accelerated speeds to reestablish contact, perhaps bearing down quickly on the Principal for identification purposes and then decelerating to establish a comfortable following distance. When the Principal stops at a traffic light or stop sign, following traffic is forced in behind. In these situations the Principal should observe for vehicles that appear to be slowing prematurely as though to avoid driving up behind him. Such occurrences provide strong indicators of surveillance to the observant Principal.

Traffic density, or lack thereof, may force a surveillance vehicle much closer to the Principal vehicle than desirable. It is not uncommon for a surveillance vehicle to find itself directly behind the Principal at a traffic stop. Such circumstances afford the Principal an excellent opportunity to examine potential surveillance vehicles and their occupants. One indicator might be a passenger-side occupant looking in his lap as though reading a map. Another might be a passenger-side occupant who is talking but does not necessarily appear to be conversing with the driver—either because his head movements are not consistent with the conversation or because the driver does not appear to be talking. This suggests that the occupant is transmitting information over a radio to other surveillance vehicles. An undisciplined surveillance operator may talk into his lap or even raise his hand and expose a communications microphone. After a potential surveillance vehicle has been forced uncomfortably close, the Principal should observe its subsequent actions. If there are supporting surveillance vehicles, it will turn off as soon as possible due to the high degree of exposure.

At dawn and at the approach of dusk, the sun can be either an asset or a liability to the surveillance detection effort. When traveling toward the sun there is poor forward visibility, forcing any surveillance vehicles to decrease their following distance. At the same time, while the Principal's visibility will be obstructed to the front, it will be relatively good to the rear, which may allow him to see following surveillance vehicles clearly. The surveillance team may attempt to overcome this disadvantage by establishing a command vehicle in front of the Principal. Conversely, when traveling away from the sun the Principal's visibility is obstructed to the rear.

Adverse weather conditions such as rain, sleet, or snow generally obstruct the Principal's vision. There are some advantages in that adverse conditions normally require surveillance vehicles to decrease their following distance. In the case of heavy rainfall or snow, particularly when traveling at high speeds, visibility is generally obstructed more to the front than to the rear. This may result in surveillance vehicles following at decreased distances due to poor visibility while the Principal has relatively better visibility to the rear. Rear visibility is normally clearest through the side-view mirrors. Here again, a surveillance team may attempt to overcome this limitation by placing a command vehicle in front of the Principal.

Recall from the discussion of surveillance principles and tactics (Chapter 3) that anytime the Principal vehicle stops (excluding standard traffic stops), the surveillance team will establish a box around it to ensure an effective transition to the mobile follow when it departs. With this in mind, the Principal will use any such stop as an opportunity to observe for indications of surveillance. More specifically, he will observe for one *particular indicator* and any surveillance vehicles that are left vulnerable by his unexpected stop. The indicator he will watch for is the surveillance vehicle that stops and positions itself to observe the parked Principal vehicle. In a one-vehicle surveillance this is very beneficial because one of the vehicles following within observation range of the Principal will be the surveillance vehicle, which will stop. This makes it much easier for the Principal to isolate and identify.

In a team surveillance follow, however, the surveillance vehicle that stops to observe the Principal vehicle probably will not be among those which were following within observation range.

In such a situation, the command surveillance vehicle will inform the team of the Principal's stop while continuing past the location in a natural manner. This allows another surveillance vehicle to establish more discreetly a position from which to observe the Principal vehicle. The observant Principal should still be able to observe the surveillance vehicle parking in his vicinity, unless surrounding cover is to the advantage of the surveillance team. Such a situation increases the probability that other vehicles parking in the Principal's vicinity in a manner that is not secure are merely coincidental, but he should observe any vehicle that meets this profile for additional indicators and subsequent recognition.

When stopping at any location, the Principal will observe all vehicles that pass by subsequent to the stop. Recall that the command vehicle will normally continue past the Principal vehicle to defer subsequent observation duties to a surveillance vehicle that can position itself in a more discreet manner. Additionally, any other surveillance vehicles that are too close to the stop's location to stop discreetly for an observation position must also continue past the Principal to avoid appearing suspicious. This affords the Principal a free look at the command vehicle and perhaps additional surveillance vehicles. The Principal will observe all passing vehicles for the purposes of subsequent recognition and to identify more specific indicators of surveillance, such as vehicle occupants who appear to scrutinize the Principal vehicle or a passenger-side occupant who is talking as if transmitting information over a radio or perhaps even bowing his head as though reading a map. Routine short-term stops, such as stopping at a gas station to pump fuel, offer excellent opportunities to observe for boxing surveillance vehicles.

As surveillance vehicles pass the location of the Principal's stop, they will continue ahead to the first appropriate location at which to turn off and either establish a box position or circle around to establish one along another route. The Principal should observe for any vehicle that appears to turn shortly after passing his location. As the Principal departs the stop location, he should observe for indicators of surveillance vehicles in box positions or pulling out to follow.

PASSIVE FOOT SURVEILLANCE DETECTION

Passive foot surveillance detection is conducted to identify specific indications of foot surveillance. The ultimate objective is to identify the same individual in two separate locations that are incoincidental. This method of surveillance detection is more difficult for a number of reasons. Foremost, the Principal on foot does not have the range of vision that is afforded by mirrors in a vehicle surveillance detection. The only method of observation is by line of sight, which is difficult if not impossible to disguise from possible surveillance operators. Virtually the only way to observe for following surveillance operators is to turn and look to the rear. This makes it much easier for the surveillance element to identify a Principal who is unusually observant of his surroundings.

Another disadvantage is that foot travel is less channelized. Vehicular surveillance is restricted to established roadways, whereas foot surveillance affords surveillance operators more flexibility in travel. This flexibility is further enhanced beyond that of vehicular surveillance because foot operators can maneuver in any direction with equal speed and security while vehicles are extremely restricted in their maneuverability.

The best opportunity for foot surveillance detection through passive observation is during the stakeout or box phases. During a foot stakeout the surveillance operators' greatest concern is adequate cover to man a box position securely while effectively observing a specified location. A vehicle parked on the side of the road with operators inside is even more plausible than a person standing out in the open for no apparent reason. For this reason, foot surveillance operators will attempt to maximize existing cover while on stakeout. The longer the duration of the Principal's stop, the longer they must remain static or reconnoitre the location. Anyone who is standing around for no discernible reason should be readily apparent to the observant Principal. In most circumstances, people on foot are moving with a purpose or destination. Those who are not are easily isolated from the surrounding populace. Such individuals should be observed for retention purposes and to identify other indications of foot surveillance.

When departing a possible stakeout location, the Principal

should focus on locations that would provide surveillance operators with their needed cover. Such locations include phone booths, bus stops, and outside shops or newsstands. The circumstances of the Principal's activities will determine how much time is available to observe surroundings. Surveillance operators transition into cover positions as an operational necessity and therefore may not appear completely natural with the activity that is used as cover. At a point, identifying an individual who appears out of place becomes an almost intuitive perception. This applies throughout all phases of foot surveillance detection.

Anyone using a pay phone, for instance, should be observed to determine whether his actions and mannerisms are consistent with that activity or are more focused on observing the surroundings. This applies to the observation of virtually any activity. People who are casually window shopping should receive particular scrutiny because this is a very shallow cover that is easily detected. Individuals waiting at a bus stop should be observed if the circumstances of the Principal's activities allow continuous observation or the opportunity to recheck the location periodically. In this case the Principal will observe for any individuals who remain at the stop after one or more buses have stopped to pick up passengers.

Foot surveillance teams operating without body communications equipment will use visual signals to communicate among each other. Visual signals will normally reflect mannerisms or actions that would appear natural to the casual observer, such as scratching the head, checking the watch, or removing a handkerchief from the pocket. The Principal will observe for individuals who display idiosyncrasies that are indicative of visual communications signals.

Foot operators wearing body communications equipment may display awkward actions and mannerisms that to the observant Principal can be indicative of surveillance. To conceal their equipment, foot operators may wear baggy or loose-fitting clothing that is not consistent with their overall build. Body communications equipment is operated by the use of a key button for transmitting. The most common place for this button is inside the operator's pocket, so the Principal should observe for individuals with their hands in their pockets or who periodically insert and remove a hand. Since communications equipment is normally worn on the upper body, surveillance operators may periodically adjust it for comfort and concealment. The equipment will include an earpiece, which the operator may need to readjust by raising a finger to the ear. Earpieces with a wire connection running down the back of the neck are readily detectable and therefore will rarely be used unless concealed by hair or another means.

Communications equipment will also include a microphone, which will be concealed under the clothing and positioned near the center of the chest. Even though the microphone is sensitive enough to pick up an operator's speech regardless of the position of his head, he may still have a tendency to lower the chin toward the chest when communicating. Yet another tendency is for the operator to stop moving and stare aimlessly when listening to radio transmissions. Experienced operators are capable of disguising the fact that they are speaking over the communications system, but the Principal should still observe for individuals who appear to be talking without reason. Recall that surveillance operators can communicate via concealed equipment without actually talking by transmitting static clicks in response to another surveillance operator's questions.

Observation of clothing and mannerisms was addressed in Chapter 4. During the course of passive surveillance detection, the Principal will rarely be close enough to a surveillance operator to distinguish specific facial features for retention and subsequent recognition. For this reason, the observation of clothing and mannerisms, which can be observed at a greater distance, will be particularly important. Observation for disguise and mannerisms was also addressed in Chapter 4. The Principal should remain constantly aware that surveillance operators will alter their appearance and mannerisms to defeat the surveillance detection effort, and he should employ the measures addressed in Chapter 4 to detect the use of disguise.

When departing or passing through a possible stakeout location, the Principal should observe for individuals who transition from a static to mobile status. This involves a consciously developed perceptive process of observing surroundings and isolating individuals who move from static positions. Through concentration and the filtering out of all unnecessary distracters, the "mind's eye" perceives movements that would normally be beyond the Principal's peripheral vision limitations. This enhanced perceptive acuity, coupled with concentrated hearing, can assist in detecting individuals who exit an establishment after the Principal passes by, as might be indicative of a surveillance operator manning a box position inside an establishment and maneuvering for the pick-up.

Since passive foot surveillance detection involves only those observations made during the course of standard travel, the Principal will have few natural opportunities to observe to the rear for surveillance operators when traveling. Virtually the only opportunity for observation of following individuals is when the Principal stops for traffic at an intersection to either continue straight or make a turn. Except in stakeouts and in public locations, a foot surveillance team is most vulnerable to detection when the Principal turns.

Figure 5 depicts a surveillance operator following directly behind the Principal on the same side of the street. The surveillance operator in this situation is only detectable by passive observation when the Principal stops at an intersection to negotiate traffic to make a turn and cross the road. As the Principal turns to negotiate traffic, it may be possible for him to observe following individuals through peripheral vision or by a slight glance to the side.

Figure 6 depicts a surveillance operator following at a distance on the opposite side of the road. Again, the surveillance operator is only detectable by passive observation when the Principal stops at an intersection to negotiate traffic to make a turn and cross the road. In this situation the surveillance operator is much more vulnerable to observation than in the previous example because the Principal will have a better field of view in this direction. As the Principal turns to negotiate traffic, he can observe pedestrians who are approaching the intersection on the opposite side. At this point, the Principal should observe in particular for individuals who either slow their pace to avoid crossing his path or quicken their pace to complete the intersection prior to his crossing. The possibility that a surveillance operator may stop suddenly, move abruptly to enter an establishment, or duck behind a physical structure for concealment cannot be discounted, but such reactions are not characteristic of a disciplined operator.

Figure 7 depicts the standard tandem surveillance positioning for two surveillance operators. Both surveillance operators are observable when the Principal stops at an intersection to negotiate traffic to make a turn and cross the road. This is accomplished through a combination of the tactics addressed in the previous two figures.

Figure 8 depicts a tandem surveillance positioning for two surveillance operators when following a Principal in dense pedestrian traffic. The operator following on the same side of the street as the Principal is detectable by the tactics detailed in Figure 5 when the Principal stops at intersection to make a turn. In this situation, however, the operator following on the opposite side of the

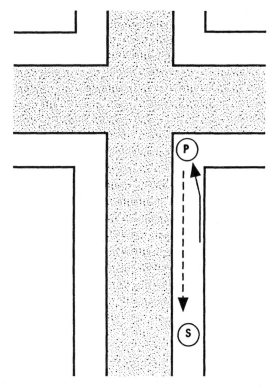

FIGURE 5

Here the surveillance operator following directly behind the Principal is detectable only by passive observation when the Principal turns and can make use of his peripheral vision or glances to the side.

street is much more vulnerable to detection because he will be caught more directly in the Principal's field of vision if he has no plausible cover under which to stop in reaction to the Principal's actions. This can occur even when the Principal continues straight at the intersection. The operator on the opposite side of the road, continuing straight to appear natural, may move up within the field of vision, making himself more vulnerable to observation.

When the Principal stops during the course of standard foot travels, he will observe for surrounding individuals who appear to transition from a mobile to static status. As the Principal approaches the location of the stop he should observe all individuals already in the area and eliminate them from primary consideration as surveillance operators. He can then focus on those who subsequently appear in static positions and who were not in

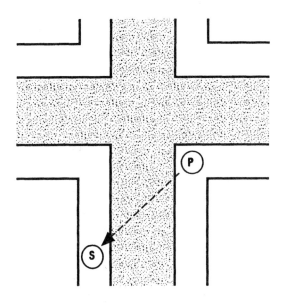

FIGURE 6

Here the surveillance operator is following at a distance on the opposite side of the road and is much more vulnerable than in the previous illustration. Again, he is only detectable by passive observation when the Principal stops to make a turn, but in this case the principle has a much better field of view.

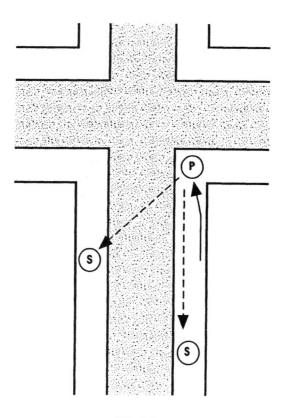

FIGURE 7

The standard tandem surveillance positioning for two surveillance operators.

the area when he made the stop. The Principal will also observe for individuals who meet the profile of a surveillance operator as addressed in the section on foot stakeouts in Chapter 3.

Passive surveillance detection in public locations is extremely effective in identifying indications of surveillance as well as specific surveillance operators. In fact, public locations are among the points in a foot surveillance operation where operators are most vulnerable to detection. Since many of the passive observation principles applicable to public locations are similar to those involved in active detection, they will not be addressed at this point. One point of note regarding public locations is that any time the Principal enters a public location, the surveillance team

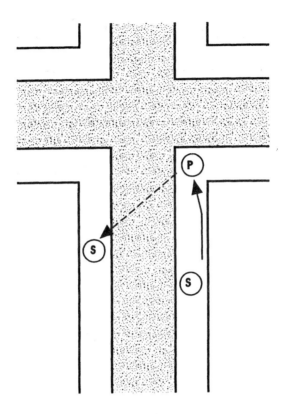

FIGURE 8
Tandem surveillance positioning for two surveillance operators when following a Principal in dense pedestrian traffic.

will establish a surveillance box outside the location to reestablish the mobile follow when he departs. For this reason, when departing a public location, the Principal will employ the same passive observation tactics as addressed previously for the foot stakeout box.

The conduct of passive foot surveillance at night incorporates specific factors that are characteristic of darkness. Observation is significantly limited at night. This affects both the Principal and the surveillance effort. Chapter 4 addressed some techniques that can be used to minimize the physiological effects of darkness. Although surveillance detection is limited somewhat under such circumstances, the Principal can exploit the limitations that darkness also imposes on the surveillance team.

Despite the enhanced degree of concealment that darkness provides the surveillance team, the hours of darkness are almost exclusively characterized by less pedestrian traffic. This decreases the degree of cover available, which in effect enables the Principal to isolate surveillance operators for detection.

Recall that observation is not limited to the sense of sight. In darkness, the sense of hearing facilitates observation because sight is obstructed while sound is enhanced due to a generally quieter environment. Additionally, due to physiological factors, when one or more of the body's senses are impaired, perception of the others is intensified in order to compensate for the degradation of the others. For these reasons, the sense of hearing enhances surveillance detection at night. Due to the physiological factors noted, the sense of smell may also enhance observation at night. A surveillance team may employ night observation devices to overcome the effects of darkness. Night observation devices either magnify existing illumination for enhanced vision or generate their own light source through an infrared beam. Any night vision device will emit light at the source through the eyepiece unless measures are taken for concealment. In creating their own light source, infrared night vision devices emit a red beam. This beam is almost undetectable, but a dull red light appears when shone directly into the eyes of an individual. The Principal can detect the use of an active night vision capability under these circumstances.

PASSIVE DETECTION OF COMBINED VEHICULAR AND FOOT SURVEILLANCE

When the Principal stops and parks his vehicle, he will observe for the indicators of surveillance as addressed in the previous section on vehicular surveillance detection. When the Principal stops to park and get out of his vehicle to travel by foot, he will also employ passive detection measures that are unique to the transition from a vehicular surveillance to a foot surveillance. The main thing the Principal should concentrate on is the fact that the surveillance team will attempt to maintain a continuity of observation during this transition.

The surveillance team will attempt to place foot operators on the ground as quickly as possible. This is a difficult task to accomplish without coming to the attention of the Principal. At this point the Principal should observe for possible foot operators exiting vehicles. In an effort to find secure locations to drop foot operators, surveillance vehicles may reconnoitre the Principal's location, making them vulnerable to detection. The Principal will continue to observe for these indicators after he has departed the location of his vehicle because the surveillance team may continue to drop foot operators anywhere along the Principal's identified route of travel. As the Principal travels by foot, he will employ the passive detection measures addressed previously with regard to passive foot surveillance detection.

As the Principal heads back to his vehicle, he will observe for indications that the surveillance team is preparing to reestablish vehicular surveillance. During this transition phase, surveillance vehicles may attempt to pick up foot operators. The Principal will observe for individuals who enter vehicles in an unnatural manner or location. Again, the Principal will observe for vehicles that appear to be surveying the area, either in an effort to find foot operators or to establish a box position. As the Principal approaches his vehicle, enters the vehicle, and pulls out to drive away, he will observe for indicators of a stakeout box as discussed in the section on the stakeout phase of vehicular surveillance detection.

The factors of less traffic on the roads, better observation of vehicle lights, and an enhanced sense of hearing are the ones to focus on in detecting the transition from vehicular to foot surveillance at night. In desolate areas this transition is extremely difficult for a surveillance team to execute discreetly. In almost any environment, surveillance vehicles are more readily detectable as they maneuver to transition foot operators to the ground. Additionally, the detection of boxing surveillance vehicles by both sight and sound is enhanced as the Principal exits his vehicle and enjoys a 360-degree observation range.

Specific indicators of surveillance include the sound of doors shutting and perhaps the observation of interior vehicle lights as surveillance operators exit vehicles. In open terrain or in close proximity to a surveillance vehicle, radio transmissions may be audible as surveillance operators get out of the vehicles. A poorly disciplined surveillance vehicle may turn off its lights for enhanced concealment while maneuvering but disregard the fact that the reverse and brake lights will still activate.

PASSIVE DETECTION OF PROGRESSIVE SURVEILLANCE

Recall from the discussion of progressive surveillance in Chapter 3 that this is the most secure method of surveillance. For this reason it is the most difficult to detect. Due to the nature of progressive surveillance, it should only be detectable by passive observation because of the security measures incorporated to preclude the effectiveness of active surveillance detection tactics.

Target pattern analysis conducted by the Principal will identify specific routes or patterns of travel that are susceptible to progressive surveillance. This analysis will assist in focusing surveillance detection observation at appropriate locations.

There are two types of progressive surveillance—mobile and fixed. Mobile progressive surveillance is initiated through the use of a stakeout box or position. Since progressive surveillance concentrates on a phased coverage of travel along established routes, stakeout boxes in support of these operations may be positioned anywhere along a given route, and not necessarily in what would normally be assessed as standard stakeout locations. This is where the pattern analysis process will assist in the detection of progressive surveillance. The Principal will identify specific routes of travel that would be of interest to a progressive surveillance effort. He will then determine appropriate stakeout locations along those routes.

As the Principal travels through possible mobile progressive surveillance stakeout locations, he will observe for indications of surveillance vehicles or operators in box positions. As with the detection of a standard stakeout to pick-up phase transition, the Principal will observe for possible surveillance vehicles that pull out to establish a mobile follow. When traveling by foot he will observe for the indicators of a foot stakeout box. Due to the restricted duration of the mobile progressive surveillance follow, there will probably be few of the indicators of mobile surveillance addressed earlier regarding vehicular and foot surveillance detection.

Both mobile and fixed progressive surveillance employ the

concept of decision points, which are locations that give the Principal the option to turn or continue straight. The most common decision points are street intersections. A fixed progressive surveillance operation is composed of static observation points established at designated decision points. Since this involves no surveillance assets traveling with the Principal, few of the surveillance detection vulnerabilities addressed throughout this chapter exist. Again, the detection of fixed progressive surveillance is driven by the target pattern analysis process. The Principal will identify possible decision points where fixed surveillance assets may be located. When approaching and passing through identified decision points, the Principal will observe for vehicles or foot operators in fixed surveillance positions.

PASSIVE SURVEILLANCE DETECTION ON PUBLIC TRANSPORTATION

Most modes of public transportation require a surveillance team to employ modified foot surveillance tactics. This is necessary because foot surveillance always precedes or resumes when the Principal either enters or exits public transportation. With the exception of the taxi cab follow, a standard vehicular surveillance cannot be conducted on public transportation systems due to their unique methods of movement. When modes of transportation follow an established route and schedule, the surveillance team will use this information to anticipate the Principal's travels.

As the Principal waits at a bus stop with the intention of boarding a bus, he should observe people who reach the bus stop after he has. Although they may be surveillance operators, a tactically sound surveillance team will attempt to either have an operator board the bus prior to the Principal or at one of the stops after his. This makes the appearance of a surveillance operator less suspicious. As the Principal enters the bus he should observe the passengers—particularly those seated to the rear. He should also observe people who board at subsequent stops. Ideally, a surveillance operator will attempt to sit to the rear of the bus in order to observe the Principal, thus preventing observation by the Principal, who is facing forward when seated. As passengers enter the bus, the Principal should observe for individuals who select seats in the rear while foregoing more convenient available seats.

A surveillance operator will remain on the bus until after the Principal has exited if there are other surveillance assets in support. For this reason, anyone who exits the bus at stops prior to the Principal's can be eliminated as possible surveillance operators. The exception to this rule is when the Principal is traveling to the last stop on the specified route. In this situation the surveillance operator will exit the bus at the next-to-last stop to avoid getting off the bus at the last stop with the Principal. A surveillance team will assume that the Principal will exit before or at the last stop, because, if he intended to travel to a stop prior to the one at which he entered the bus, it would have been more logical to have taken a bus that traveled in the opposite direction. Therefore, when traveling to the last stop on the route, the Principal should be particularly observant of passengers who exit at the next-to-last stop. Obviously, the Principal should also be observant of those who exit the bus at the same stop as he does.

There are unique tactics involved with the vehicular surveillance of a bus when the Principal is a passenger because a standard vehicular surveillance follow is not secure due to the bus' frequent stops. Based on a knowledge of the bus' route, the surveillance team will concentrate on the forward positioning of surveillance vehicles to have surveillance operators available to take to the ground for a foot follow immediately upon the Principal's exit. This requires that surveillance vehicles maneuver ahead of the bus to establish their positions. When there are few surveillance vehicles involved or there are too many bus stops to be covered, surveillance vehicles may be forced to pass the bus more than once during the course of the route. The Principal should therefore be observant of vehicles that meet this profile.

As the Principal exits the bus he should observe for indications of a foot stakeout or the transition to a foot surveillance. When the Principal takes a bus to a specific location, it is a logical assumption that he will return to the same bus stop for the return trip after the purpose of his travels is concluded. The surveillance team will operate under this assumption while the Principal is on the ground, particularly if it loses sight of the Principal during the conduct of the foot surveillance. For this reason, the Principal should observe for indications of a stakeout box when returning to the bus stop.

Passive surveillance detection on subways and commuter trains employs many of the same concepts addressed with public bus travel. Generally, the density of traffic associated with subway travel makes detection more difficult than with buses. One advantage in surveillance detection on the subway is that a surveillance team will attempt to place multiple operators on the Principal's train, although not all operators will be within observation range of the Principal. Surveillance operators on the train will invariably disembark at the same location as the Principal.

Passive surveillance detection tactics are similar for both ticketed bus and ticketed train travel. In these cases, a surveillance team will likely make an effort to determine in advance the Principal's travel itinerary. When he makes his travel arrangements at the station just prior to travel, a surveillance operator should be close enough to the ticket window to overhear the transaction as the Principal purchases his ticket. For this reason, the Principal should note and commit to memory any individual who may be, explicably or not, within hearing range of the transaction. This concept is also applicable to airplane travel when the Principal is either purchasing a ticket or checking in his luggage.

When traveling on a train or bus, the Principal should observe all individuals for subsequent recognition. Many trains are compartmented, which will assist in the isolation of potential surveillance operators, but bear in mind that possible operators on the train are not limited to those traveling within observation range of the Principal. Longer rides will give the Principal more opportunities to identify individuals who may be giving him more attention than is warranted or appear conspicuous in some other way.

In some circumstances, a surveillance team may select to place a surveillance operator "up against" the Principal. This refers to the tactic of actually having a surveillance operator establish contact and rapport with the Principal, taking advantage of the natural occurrence of chance contacts with strangers that is characteristic of such travels. This gives the "harmless stranger" an opportunity to gain exceptional insight into the Principal's demeanor, as well as eliciting information that may be of value to the surveillance team.

To counter this tactic on public transportation, or any other situation in which it may occur, the Principal will be particularly sensitive to such encounters and guard against providing information to anyone. Innocuous individuals, such as senior citizens or women disguised to be pregnant, are commonly used for this purpose because their appearance alone will normally allow them to bypass the Principal's defenses. It is necessary to observe the individual involved in any such chance encounter carefully, although if he is actually a surveillance operator he will never be seen again, unless the surveillance team is particularly inept.

The exception to this is when the surveillance team intends to employ an individual to establish a continued relationship as a source of information on the Principal. The Principal should always be suspicious of people who are immediately able to establish rapport in chance encounters based on a common professional or personal interest. Any attempts by such individuals to arrange further contact with the Principal should be regarded with extreme caution, as should any coincidental chance encounter that occurs at a later date.

As the Principal disembarks the train or bus, he should observe for indications of a surveillance box and the subsequent pick-up.

CHAPTER 6

ACTIVE PHYSICAL SURVEILLANCE DETECTION OVERVIEW

Active physical surveillance detection consists of specific, normally preplanned maneuvers executed by the Principal to elicit a reaction from a surveillance asset. By orchestrating an unanticipated situation to which the surveillance asset must react, the Principal isolates that asset for identification. As with passive detection, active physical surveillance detection is based on knowledge of how a surveillance team operates. Such an understanding allows the Principal to employ active measures that will invoke compromising actions by surveillance assets.

Active surveillance detection is employed when the Principal has identified specific indicators of surveillance. The Principal will execute surveillance detection maneuvers to confirm any suspicions. He may also use active physical surveillance as a standard security practice prior to conducting protected activity. This allows the Principal to confirm the absence of surveillance before conducting any activity that would be damaging to him if observed by surveillance. The most common practitioners of active surveillance detection are espionage agents, who will engage in extensive detection drills prior to any operational meetings or activities.

Active surveillance detection is dependent on the principles of observation for success. No surveillance detection maneuver is effective in exposing surveillance unless the Principal is in position to observe the reaction. Active surveillance detection will rarely expose surveillance with each maneuver. In most cases, the Principal will at best develop specific indicators to focus on for observation and retention. For instance, although a surveillance detection maneuver may elicit a suspicious reaction from a nearby vehicle, it is normally not until that vehicle is observed subsequently at an incoincidental location that surveillance can be confirmed.

There are two methods of active physical surveillance detection: overt and discreet. The Principal will use the overt method when he is not concerned that surveillance detection tactics will be identified as such. Overt surveillance detection tactics are generally associated with overt targets (as defined in Chapter 2). Although it is usually in the Principal's interest to disguise the fact that surveillance detection tactics are being employed, at times the need to determine for certain whether surveillance is present may override these considerations. For example, protective security personnel employing surveillance detection for executive protection purposes will be extremely overt in attempting to detect surveillance.

Discreet physical surveillance detection tactics are employed in a manner that disguises the use of detection measures. It is always to the Principal's advantage if a surveillance team does not identify surveillance detection measures for the very reasons addressed in the previous chapter. Overt detection tactics generally involve more aggressive maneuvers designed to provoke a more conspicuous reaction. In relative terms, the more overt the surveillance detection maneuver, the more effective it will be in exposing surveillance. Overall, active physical surveillance detection maneuvers range from discreet to extremely overt, with many degrees in between.

The negative impact that overt tactics can have on the overall effectiveness of the detection effort should influence the selection of the method of surveillance detection. Although overt maneuvers may be effective in forcing a suspicious reaction from a surveillance asset, they will rarely *confirm* surveillance in and of themselves. A primary objective of surveillance detection is to isolate a surveillance asset for observation, retention, and subsequent recognition. When a surveillance asset assesses that it has received a high degree of exposure to the Principal due to an overt surveillance detection maneuver, the particular vehicle or operator at issue may be called off the operation. This deprives the Principal of an opportunity to confirm surveillance by observing that asset at a subsequent time and location.

SURVEILLANCE COMMUNICATIONS DETECTION

A surveillance team depends on communications for a secure and coordinated effort. Most operationally capable surveillance teams will depend on radio communications equipment during all aspects of its surveillance operations. The communications equipment a team may employ ranges from hand-held radios to discreetly installed vehicular communications systems. Regardless of the degree of sophistication, all radio communications systems transmit radio frequency signals into the atmosphere. Although in most cases this is a surveillance team's greatest vulnerability to detection, it must be accepted because of the importance of a communications capability.

The Principal should acquire the equipment needed to capitalize on the vulnerabilities inherent in surveillance communications. Rather than getting involved with more sophisticated communications detection equipment, however, radio frequency scanners are all that should be necessary. A limitation of commercially purchased frequency scanners is that they are designed to monitor only those frequencies authorized by federal regulations. A surveillance team concerned with the vulnerability of communications to frequency scanners will operate on radio frequencies outside the range of standard scanning equipment. In fact, many federal restrictions regulating the use and monitoring of certain frequency ranges are in place to protect the security of law enforcement and intelligence operations such as surveillance.

Commercial frequency scanners can be modified to receive restricted frequencies with some research. This information is available in various electronics publications. Electronics enthusiasts with this and other knowledge are not difficult to find. It is worthwhile to establish a relationship with an employee of an electronics equipment business. Once one has established rapport, such individuals are excellent sources of information regarding technical equipment applications and the frequencies used in a given area for particular purposes.

Two frequency scanners are ideal for surveillance detection purposes. A fixed scanner should be used in the residence to monitor activity in the general vicinity. This is probably the most effective means of detecting surveillance communications because much of a surveillance operation is based around the Principal's residence. From this location the Principal can discreetly dedicate the necessary time to scan the spectrum and identify communications activity of interest. He should also use a mobile scanner when traveling by vehicle. This is most effective when used to monitor frequencies or frequency ranges that have been identified to be of interest through fixed scanning efforts.

Surveillance teams may use encrypted communications to maintain the security of their activities. Encrypted, or encoded, communications are scrambled in a manner that restricts their reception to radios that are programmed to decrypt the transmissions. The technology does exist to decrypt scrambled transmissions, but such a capability is beyond the expertise and financial means of most people. Encrypted communications are effective in protecting specific information regarding a surveillance operation, but they are as vulnerable to detection as unsecured transmissions. When encrypted communications transmit over the radio's frequency, only static can be received by a radio that is not programmed for decryption. Although this protects the actual details of the conversation, it does reveal the fact that the frequency is being used for communications.

When a scanner locks onto a frequency that transmits only intermittent rushes of static, this should be viewed as an initial indication of encrypted surveillance communications. If the signal is weak and only static is received, then the signal is probably on the fringe of the scanner's range. Signals that are generated from this distance are not indicative of surveillance due to their distance from the scanning activity. However, strong static signals are a significant indicator of encrypted surveillance communications. When a possible encrypted frequency is identified, the Principal will program this frequency into the mobile scanner for confirmation purposes. As the Principal travels by vehicle he will monitor the frequency for activity. If the static transmissions correspond to the activities of the Principal, then surveillance is confirmed. An example of this is when a rush of static is transmitted every time the Principal makes a turn, indicating that a surveillance vehicle is informing the team of this activity.

SURVEILLANCE DETECTION PLANNING AND TARGET PATTERN ANALYSIS

As with passive detection, active physical surveillance detection uses the concept of target pattern analysis. The analysis process will be initiated as addressed in the previous chapter. The Principal will evaluate his own activities and travel patterns to determine how a surveillance team would employ coverage. Based on this concept of the surveillance strategy, he will identify those specific locations where active detection methods can be employed with the highest probability of success. The pattern analysis process will continue beyond that conducted in support of passive detection by actually identifying routes of travel and specific terrain characteristics along those routes that will facilitate active detection maneuvers. As specific detection tactics are addressed in subsequent chapters, the principle of advantageous terrain will become apparent.

To conduct discreet active physical surveillance detection effectively, the Principal must develop specific surveillance detection maneuvers based on established patterns of activity. Recall that the target pattern analysis process is based on the assumption that the surveillance team has made sufficient observations of the Principal's travels and activities to develop a comprehensive picture of his standard patterns. Surveillance detection practices involving activities that are significantly inconsistent with these established patterns will be readily apparent to a surveillance team if present. Therefore, it is necessary to develop specific surveillance maneuvers that are consistent with established patterns. The Principal's target pattern analysis will ensure that surveillance detection practices meet this criterion.

This is a particularly important concept because it enables the Principal to use the target pattern analysis the surveillance team has conducted in support of its operation against it. A surveillance team generally becomes more efficient and effective against a Principal after it has observed him for a period of time and has become familiar with the activities and travels incorporated into the pattern analysis process. This allows the team to better anticipate the Principal's intentions. For example, if the Principal establishes a pattern of leaving the workplace at a standard time and traveling directly home by a specific route, the surveillance team will anticipate this activity and coordinate its surveillance coverage accordingly. Even though the surveillance team will be prepared to react to unanticipated travels, it will instinctively assume that the Principal will conform to the previously established pattern. This can work against the surveillance team from the active surveillance detection standpoint, because the team will tend to develop a sense of security by relying on established patterns to dictate its coverage strategy. When this sense of security is suddenly disrupted by an unanticipated maneuver on the part of the Principal, the team may be forced to react in a manner that leaves it vulnerable to detection.

A Principal with a wide and varied pattern of activities and travels has much more latitude with which to incorporate natural active surveillance detection measures than one with a relatively restricted pattern. Most people conform to the latter because they are restricted by a standard day-to-day routine. The more active someone is in his travels and activities, the more the pattern is expanded. If the Principal determines through target pattern analysis that his patterns are too narrow in scope to accommodate the necessary surveillance detection activities, he should make a conscious effort to gradually expand them. This is accomplished by making activities more frequent and varied, such as going to a different location for lunch every day or varying the route of travel home from work. In doing so, however, the Principal must ensure that a plausible reason for the variation is apparent in case surveillance is present. For example if varying the route home from work, a plausible reason might be a stop at a different store when appropriate.

Active physical surveillance detection can be either preplanned or spontaneous. During the course of travel the Principal may identify indicators of surveillance and determine a need to conduct it to confirm any suspicions. Such spontaneous surveillance detection measures are more difficult to conduct discreetly due to the general lack of preparation and planning. Active surveillance detection is always more effective when the maneuvers and locations of execution are planned in advance.

Active surveillance detection is based on the Principal conducting a maneuver that elicits a reaction and exposes a surveillance asset. To this end, the planning of surveillance detection maneuvers must always take into consideration the anticipated or desired reaction of the surveillance asset if present. This allows the maneuvers to be assessed in advance as to their effectiveness in satisfying the objective and whether their effectiveness offsets the risk involved in conducting them. The risk involved consists of the probability that surveillance assets, if present, will identify the fact that the Principal is conducting active surveillance detection against them. In determining the effectiveness of a surveillance detection maneuver, the Principal must factor in his ability to observe the desired surveillance reaction. Obviously, the best-executed surveillance detection maneuver is ineffective if the Principal is unable to observe the surveillance asset's reaction to it. The aforementioned considerations emphasize the importance of preparation and planning in surveillance detection practices.

Area knowledge is necessary for the effective execution of active surveillance detection measures. It is critical to the success of spontaneous surveillance detection, because in order to conduct surveillance detection without preparation, the Principal must be familiar with available terrain that facilitates such efforts. Area familiarization directs the planning of active surveillance detection activities. The Principal must be intimately aware of traffic patterns throughout the area and how these patterns will affect the surveillance detection effort. Traffic patterns include traffic density, the authorized speed limits on various routes of travel, and traffic control measures such as traffic lights, one-way roads, and toll booths. Area familiarization should also include the items addressed in the previous chapter.

SURVEILLANCE DETECTION ROUTES

A surveillance detection route (SDR) is one around which the formalized detection plan is based. The previously addressed concepts of surveillance detection planning and target pattern analysis are the basis for the SDR. An SDR will consist of a logical route of travel that maximizes existing terrain and traffic characteristics to incorporate surveillance detection measures. The primary reason for developing an SDR is to ensure that surveillance detection activities are well conceived and follow a logical pattern of travel.

In some cases the development of an SDR may be the only active measure taken in regard to surveillance detection. To this end, the SDR may simply involve a route that enhances the effectiveness of passive observation and detection activities. The most basic example of this type of SDR is the "three sides of a box" route. This involves the Principal traveling a route that follows three sides of boxed terrain, such as a city block, and observing for any individual who follows this illogical route.

Figure 9 depicts how traveling through points A, B, and C, to point D is an illogical route, given the option of traveling directly

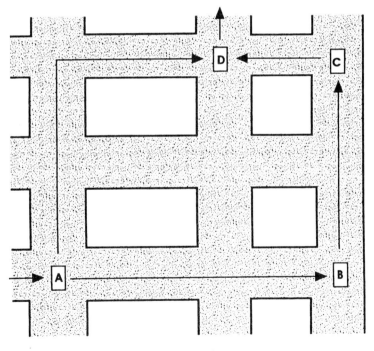

FIGURE 9
How the "three sides of a box route" works.

from point A to point D. Although this simple example of an SDR may be easily identified as such, there are many routes that can incorporate three sides of a box that are not as easily recognizable. An excellent time for the Principal to execute this type of SDR is when he has lured a possible vehicular surveillance team to unfamiliar terrain and then departs the vehicle by foot. At this point the foot surveillance operators may follow the Principal more readily through three sides of a box because they have little knowledge of the area.

In most cases an SDR will incorporate active surveillance detection maneuvers throughout. Programmed maneuvers will be executed in locations that maximize observation of surrounding traffic at their point of execution. The objective of such an SDR is to execute sequential surveillance detection maneuvers that will identify suspicious vehicles or individuals initially and subsequently confirm their identities as surveillance assets.

CHAPTER 7

ACTIVE STAKEOUT AND OBSERVATION POST DETECTION MEASURES

The stakeout is the phase of a surveillance operation in which the surveillance team is most vulnerable to detection. Here the team must establish basically static positions for extended periods of time with a degree of uncertainty regarding exactly when and where the Principal will emerge initially. The Principal will take advantage of this in the employment of surveillance detection measures. He will use the target pattern analysis process extensively in stakeout detection.

OBSERVATION POST DETECTION

A surveillance team may employ an observation post (see Chapter 3) either for a fixed surveillance of a specified location or as a trigger in support of the mobile surveillance stakeout. An observation post serves a very important purpose in support of the stakeout because it provides a secure position from which to observe a location without having to expose a surveillance vehicle or operator. It allows the surveillance team to observe a location around the clock without requiring that the entire team remain on stakeout during hours of limited activity, such as at night. Whether the observation post serves the purpose of a fixed surveillance or it is used in support of a stakeout, it will consist of the same characteristics.

The primary location for the employment of an observation post will be at the Principal's residence or workplace. The fact that the observation post will be based to observe the exterior of a denied area is a major factor the Principal will exploit in detection. Be it a residence, a workplace, or a similar location, the Principal will have free access to the interior of the denied area while the surveillance team is generally restricted from observing inside.

Through analysis, the Principal will determine which locations a surveillance team may target through the use of an observation post. The Principal will first determine the specific location around the area which the surveillance team would prioritize focus. Normally, the primary objective of an observation post around a residence is to observe the Principal enter his vehicle and drive away. So it is logical to assume that an observation post would be in position to observe the vehicle or the garage door. An observation post will also attempt to observe the primary exit the Principal is expected to use when departing the location. Observation posts may also be positioned so surveillance operators can observe activities inside location windows.

In residential areas it is relatively easy to isolate possible observation post locations through the process of elimination. Although law enforcement or national investigative agencies may commission the cooperation of a neighbor to set up an observation post, this is rarely done. In a residential area where the Principal knows the neighbors, or is at least aware of who resides at specific residences, it is easy to eliminate locations as possible observation posts. In apartment complexes or commercial areas, the Principal should be able to identify a number of possible locations for observation posts. When he has done so, the Principal will begin to observe the observers.

The Principal will identify a location from which he can observe the suspected observation post. An attic that affords outside observation is normally best for this purpose. Whatever location is chosen, it should be one that would not be a primary focus of surveillance observation. Assume that the surveillance team knows the layout of the location and is aware of which areas within should be the most active. The Principal will analyze the surveillance team's focus and position himself in a location that is not consistent with that focus. The area should be void of any light that will provide a silhouette to observers. Windows to the location should be concealed by heavy fabric or double-layered curtains to deter observation by image-enhancing optical equipment. The Principal should use a slight divide in the center of the curtains at the base of the window or one in either side of the window frame for outside observation. This process can be lengthy and most often frustrating, requiring much patience.

An observation post will share many of the same principles of concealment mentioned in the previous paragraph. Surveillance operators manning an observation post will remain concealed inside the location to avoid any exposure to the Principal. Therefore, the Principal may detect such locations based on their conspicuous inactivity. Any rooms of a possible observation post that are illuminated at night can be eliminated. The Principal should observe for specific rooms that remain concealed during the day. By eliminating some rooms and identifying others as possible observation post locations in this way, the Principal can then focus on future detection practices.

The same surveillance operators cannot remain inside a constant observation post indefinitely. Eventually observation post teams will exchange duties, leaving themselves vulnerable to detection. This exchange will normally take place in the middle of the night, even when it may seem more likely that this would occur during the day when the Principal is away. The reason for this is that the surveillance team is not only trying to avoid drawing the attention of the Principal but also that of neighbors who may become suspicious of unusual activity.

More aggressive active measures to be employed in the detection of observation posts include the use of infrared-detecting equipment to determine whether the opposition is using infrared devices. Another active measure is to have an anonymous package delivered to a suspected location with instructions to leave it at the door if there is no answer. This action may draw a surveillance operator to the door for observation, but it is likely that surveillance operators will leave the package in place and remain concealed. The Principal will then continue constant observation of the package because a surveillance operator will eventually emerge, probably under the concealment of darkness, and remove the package to restore a more natural appearance to the observation post location.

Even more aggressive measures include reporting an emergency, such as a civil disturbance, at the suspected observation post location. Since this is illegal, the Principal should ensure that the distress call cannot be traced to its origin. While emergency personnel respond, the Principal will observe to identify individuals occupying the location. Regardless of the result, the surveillance team will consider its observation post compromised and depart. This departure will be done without panic, in a manner which would draw no attention, and again, it will probably take place under the concealment of darkness.

Another tactic that may draw a surveillance effort into the open is to place mail in a roadside mailbox if applicable. After placing mail in his box and raising the flag to indicate that mail is inside for pick-up, the Principal will observe the mailbox from a secure location to identify anyone who attempts to inspect the contents. A poorly disciplined surveillance team may risk exposure by dispatching an operator to examine the mail. Again, any such activity will likely occur under the cover of darkness.

Mobile surveillance systems may be used as observation posts when there are no fixed structures available to provide sufficient cover. Mobile observation posts normally take the form of a passenger van similar to others common to the area. Observation post vans may also have an official designation or commercial wording on the exterior to provide a plausible reason for their being in a particular area. Vans with distinctive wording can only serve a limited purpose, however, because their extended presence will eventually appear suspicious. Mobile observation posts may also be established out of campers or trucks. A standard vehicle with remotely monitored video equipment can also be positioned as an observation post.

A mobile observation post must be able to observe a specified location while not appearing conspicuous. In areas where there is a concentration of vehicles parked on the street, it is easy to blend in. In sparsely trafficked or residential areas, remaining inconspicuous is more difficult.

A fully integrated mobile system will be equipped with observation, video, and photographic equipment. The equipment will be installed so that surveillance operators inside can monitor surrounding activity without physically observing out of the vehicle.

Many systems have a periscope built out of the top to appear as a sun roof extension, a ventilator unit, or another standard item. The vehicle will also be constructed in a manner that precludes any outside observation of the interior. The front will be completely segregated from the rear portion to prevent anyone from seeing into the rear through the windshield or front windows. The rear portion of the vehicle will either be void of windows or have windows covered by curtains, tinting, or reflective lining. To the unwitting pedestrian, this will not appear suspicious, but to the observant Principal, such characteristics will be strong indicators of an observation post vehicle.

Primary considerations for the Principal in detecting an observation post vehicle, or any surveillance vehicle for that matter, are familiarity with the vehicles that are normally in the area of the possible stakeout location and an ability to identify those that are alien. Familiarity with the indigenous vehicles will facilitate initial efforts to isolate possible observation post vehicles. The Principal will determine locations that are appropriate for the employment of an observation post vehicle. In observing for such a vehicle, he will attempt to identify those characteristics previously addressed. He will focus on any vehicle that remains in place for an extended period of time. In order to maintain a natural appearance, a surveillance operator will park the observation post vehicle and then depart, leaving it with surveillance operators who are manning the rear portion. A poorly disciplined surveillance team may park the observation vehicle and man it with the driver. If the Principal is fortunate enough to observe a driver parking a vehicle without ever departing, he will have confirmed surveillance.

In areas where parking space is at a premium, the surveillance team will park the vehicle at a time of day that affords the best selection of parking spots in order to position it in an appropriate location for observation. In many areas this will be early in the morning. The Principal should observe for vehicles that appear in the area overnight. The surveillance team may park the vehicle in a location that it subsequently determines does not provide optimum observation. Although this is a poor security practice, the team may choose to move it to another location with a better vantage point. Unless the surveillance operators are extremely cavalier, they will only do so when they are certain that the Principal is not in the area to observe them. Regardless of the security practices the team employs, the Principal should be able to identify vehicles that remain in the area but not necessarily in the same location for extended periods.

The Principal should continually observe any vehicle he suspects is an observation post. Eventually a surveillance operator will return to the vehicle to move it. Additionally, surveillance operators cannot remain in an observation post vehicle for extended periods—for sanitary reasons, if nothing else. An observation post vehicle that is parked in a good location will remain while operators are rotated out. As with the observation post, the surveillance team will rarely rotate operators during the day when the Principal is away from the area because this will appear suspicious to anyone else who may be observing. The team will normally rotate operators only at night, when the possibility of detection is at a minimum. Thus, by maintaining constant observation of a suspected observation post vehicle, the Principal may confirm surveillance by observing operators exchanging duties.

A more aggressive detection measure to be employed is to report a suspected vehicle to law enforcement authorities. The call should be made so it cannot be traced to the Principal in case the surveillance asset happens to be a law enforcement agency's. The Principal will observe as police officers approach the vehicle, possibly forcing out the surveillance operators. If the vehicle is in fact a surveillance asset but passes the scrutiny of the police inquiry, the team will nevertheless consider it compromised and move it at the first secure opportunity. If the vehicle moves without ever being approached—or at least driven past—by police officers, the Principal has confirmed that it was a law enforcement agency observation post vehicle.

STAKEOUT DETECTION

The target pattern analysis process used to determine how a surveillance team would establish a stakeout to cover a Principal is much more extensive for active physical surveillance detection. Recall that a stakeout box is emplaced to establish initial command of the Principal as he either passes through or emerges from within the stakeout box. Surveillance vehicles will be positioned to observe all routes into and out of the specified stakeout area. The positioning will enable a surveillance vehicle to pull out and establish command of the Principal to initiate the mobile follow along every route out of the stakeout area. Figure 10 depicts a stakeout box established to pick up a Principal as he drives away from a residence (R).

The surveillance vehicles (S) are shown in simplified box positions to illustrate how they would position themselves to initiate the follow as the Principal travels out of the stakeout box. The arrows in front of each surveillance vehicle indicate the direction in which they are oriented in order to pick up the Principal as he does so. Recall from Chapter 5 that surveillance

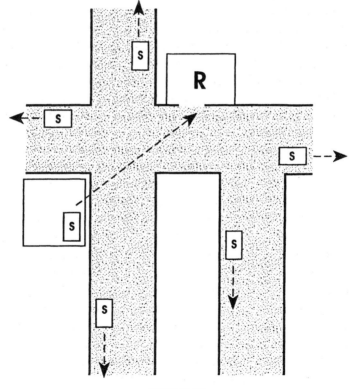

FIGURE 10

A stakeout box established for pick-up of the Principal as he drives away from his residence.

vehicles will only be positioned in this manner when there is sufficient cover from other vehicles parked on the road to ensure a relative degree of security. More secure locations for stakeout box positions include adjacent roads and parking lots, but the tactics of maneuvering to establish command of the Principal as he exits the stakeout box apply to these positions as well. The trigger vehicle (T) is parked in a concealed position that enables it to observe the residence discreetly at the locations from which Principal is expected to exit.

A surveillance stakeout may be established around a location the Principal is expected to pass through, but they are most commonly established around a denied area, such as a residence or workplace where the Principal is known or believed to be housed. A stakeout established around a location the Principal is anticipated to pass through shares the same characteristics as a surveillance box established when the Principal stops during a mobile surveillance follow. The following chapter will address the methods of active physical surveillance detection as they apply to this type of surveillance box.

The Principal will employ his knowledge of surveillance stakeout tactics to anticipate how a surveillance team will position itself. He will determine likely stakeout coverage tactics for every area he identifies as a possible stakeout location, thereby identifying where surveillance vehicles would be positioned if a surveillance stakeout is present. At this point the Principal is prepared to employ active measures of physical surveillance detection.

As the Principal leaves the location where a stakeout may be established, he will observe for a vehicle or individual meeting the profile of a trigger position. However, recall that the team may use an observation post to serve as the trigger, negating the need for a vehicle or operator to support this aspect of the operation. An appropriately placed trigger will be positioned to observe the exit to the denied location or the Principal vehicle without being visible from inside the denied area. If the trigger meets these criteria then the Principal will not have an opportunity to observe it until he has exited the denied location. Thus he has only a limited time to observe for a trigger in an inconspicuous manner.

If the Principal parks his vehicle in the garage or driveway of his residence, he should establish a pattern of always backing into the parking position. This gives him a better field of view to observe for a trigger when driving out to the street and departing. This is particularly important when the vehicle is parked in a garage that adjoins the residence, because the time between the vehicle's exiting the garage and its entering the street is virtually all he has to observe for a trigger.

The Principal should establish a pattern of locking the vehicle when it is parked in the driveway or out on the street. As he departs the residence he will discreetly observe for a trigger while approaching the vehicle. Having to unlock the vehicle gives him more time to observe.

When possible, the Principal should subscribe to a local morning newspaper and request that it be left in the yard near the street or in a mailbox at the street. By establishing a pattern of going out to get the paper and then returning to the residence about five minutes before leaving the residence for the day, the Principal creates a plausible reason for being in position to observe for a trigger. In fact, a surveillance team may welcome this activity—not realizing the actual surveillance detection purposes it serves—because it provides an indication that the Principal is preparing to leave for the day.

An appropriately established trigger should be positioned in a location away from the direction in which the Principal is expected to travel upon departing the stakeout location. This minimizes the possibility of his driving past the trigger. Ideally, from the surveillance team's standpoint, the trigger will be positioned off the road in an area such as a parking lot, but this is not always possible given the surrounding terrain. When a trigger must be parked on the street that runs in front of the denied location, it will be positioned opposite to the Principal's anticipated direction of travel. On a one-way street this is an easy judgment, but normally the trigger must determine positioning based on other factors. Target pattern analysis will be used to determine the direction in which the Principal usually departs the stakeout location, or that in which he normally departs at a given time. If the Principal parks his vehicle on the street in front of the denied location, the trigger may position itself opposite the direction in which the vehicle is facing, assuming that the Principal will depart in that direction rather than turn around.

Based on this reasoning, the Principal should avoid establishing a pattern of parking his vehicle facing the same direction every time it is parked on the street. This forces the trigger to position itself with a degree of uncertainty. If the trigger bases its position on the assumption that the Principal vehicle will depart in the direction which it is facing when parked, then the trigger is vulnerable to detection if the Principal then turns around and departs in the opposite direction. The Principal should employ this tactic when he believes there is a good probability of success. However, he should not establish a pattern of doing so, as this would only make a surveillance team suspicious, and eventually adaptive, rendering the maneuver ineffective.

A slightly overt application of this concept is initiated as the Principal approaches the possible stakeout location. Assuming that surveillance is present, the Principal will execute a U-turn to orient the vehicle in the opposite direction from which it approached and then park. Based on this action, the observing surveillance team will assume that the Principal has predetermined his next direction of travel. The Principal will then enter the stakeout location for a short period of time, but long enough for the surveillance team to maneuver its vehicles into stakeout box positions. When he exits the stakeout location, the Principal will execute a U-turn when departing by vehicle in order to detect a trigger vehicle that was positioned based on the Principal's earlier deceptive indicator of his intended direction of travel.

When the stakeout location is situated in an apartment complex, the surveillance team may have more flexibility and concealment with which to establish a trigger position. When the Principal resides at a hotel, the surveillance team may position a trigger operator inside the lobby to provide it with early warning regarding the Principal's activity and to inform it of the exit by which he is departing. When residing at a hotel, the Principal should observe for individuals in stationary positions in the lobby or other common areas.

A surveillance team may also attempt to get a room next to or on the same floor as the Principal's. Although this is normally done to support technical surveillance operations, the team will also use this placement as a trigger for the physical surveillance stakeout. An aggressive detection method that can be employed in this situation is for the Principal to stand in the hallway for a period of time after he exits and locks his room, observing for other guests who depart their room shortly after he does and identifying their room number. The Principal will focus on this room as a potential base of surveillance activity and may have a subsequent opportunity to identify the individual registered to the room. Any opportunity the Principal has to identify a surveillance operator by name enables him to detect surveillance at its source through some investigative effort.

An effective active surveillance detection measure to identify a trigger vehicle or any surveillance vehicle in a box position is for the Principal to take a walk when he anticipates that there may be a stakeout. This should be done at a time when, based on pattern analysis, the surveillance team would not anticipate such an action. The Principal will design the route to cover suspected locations where surveillance vehicles may be positioned. If he does so in a logical manner, the purpose for the walk will appear natural to the surveillance team. Even a simple walk around the neighborhood for exercise will follow a logical route rather than meandering about. It is best to incorporate a plausible destination into the walk, such as a friend's house or a nearby store.

When the stakeout is based around a home in a residential area, it is many times difficult, if not impossible, for the team to observe the rear of the residence. If the Principal establishes a pattern that leads the team to assume that he only departs from the front, which is normally the case, the team will not attempt to position a trigger to observe the rear of the house. An aggressive active measure is for the Principal to depart the denied location from the rear so that he cannot be observed by surveillance operators positioned for forward observation. By traveling back to another street without being detected by the surveillance team, the Principal can walk throughout the area to identify possible surveillance vehicles in stakeout box positions. This tactic leaves the surveillance team particularly vulnerable to detection because it will adopt a more relaxed security posture in assuming that the Principal is still inside the denied location. The Principal must exercise discretion, because if the surveillance team observes him maneuvering throughout the area after having departed the denied location covertly, it will certainly assume that he is practicing surveillance detection. If this tactic is employed under the cover of darkness it affords the Principal an additional degree of concealment.

A logical 180-degree turn is also an effective surveillance detection maneuver against the stakeout. This maneuver should be based on an analysis of where surveillance vehicles are likely to be positioned and its expected results. The Principal will depart the denied location by vehicle and drive until he believes he has broken the stakeout box. At this point, under the guise of having to return to the location, he will turn the vehicle around. He should do so by making an actual 180-degree U-turn rather than circling a block, in order to retrace the route he traveled out of the box. The objective of this doubling back is to encounter a surveillance vehicle that has left its box position to pursue him.

The Principal should observe any vehicles he encounters along the route in returning to the location. This maneuver may also elicit a suspicious reaction from the driver of a surveillance vehicle, who was surprised and left vulnerable. Possible reactions include speeding up to pass by the Principal more quickly, turning quickly onto a side street to avoid crossing paths with the Principal, or behaving unnaturally, perhaps by making too much of an effort to maintain forward focus and avoid looking in the Principal's direction. This maneuver should be concluded with an action that provides a plausible reason for the Principal's return to the location, such as locking the door or retrieving an article he forgot. (The next chapter provides more information on the 180-degree turn.)

Another aggressive detection maneuver is to depart the possible stakeout location, circle the block, and either return to the location or pass by and continue with the planned travel. This is a very overt detection measure because there is little logical reason for such a maneuver. The fact that it confounds logic is precisely why it is effective. When the surveillance team is determining box locations, it bases the positioning of operators on roads which it does not expect the Principal to use. Normally it will select one of the streets on the side of the block the stakeout is covering as a secure position, for the very reason that the

Principal would not logically circle his own block. This applies to either the block which the target location is actually on or the one on the opposite side of the street, whichever is determined to be the Principal's least likely route of departure. This maneuver also provides a good opportunity for the Principal to observe a trigger vehicle still in the box position or beginning to maneuver as the Principal passes back by.

CHAPTER 8

ACTIVE VEHICULAR SURVEILLANCE DETECTION

Active vehicular surveillance detection offers the Principal the greatest variety of detection maneuvers. During the follow phase of a surveillance operation, the team is in a reactive mode, dictated by the actions of the Principal. For a sophisticated surveillance team this is not a disadvantage because the operators are disciplined to react to virtually any maneuver in a systematic manner. It is only when the Principal maneuvers in a nonstandard manner that the surveillance team's reactions are thrown out of synchronization. This complication forces the surveillance team to rely on resourcefulness rather than its planned tactical applications. Active surveillance detection is employed to force a surveillance asset to react in an unnatural manner when encountering an unanticipated maneuver by the Principal.

Active vehicular surveillance detection should be planned and should conform to the Principal's established travel patterns. One travel pattern that enhances the ability to conduct surveillance detection is fast and aggressive driving. However, this should only be used if it conforms to the Principal's normal pattern. A Principal who drives in a conservative manner on most occasions and then drives aggressively only when intending to conduct active surveillance detection sends an undesirable signal to a surveillance team. One reason fast and aggressive driving is an advantage is that it forces the surveillance team to drive in a similar manner. When the Principal is maneuvering through traffic aggressively, it is easy to observe to the rear for vehicles that are following in a similar manner.

In relation to aggressive driving, a Principal who establishes a pattern of using expedient shortcuts such as ducking into back streets or cutting through parking lots to avoid traffic signals has more flexibility in conducting surveillance detection maneuvers. Additionally, the Principal who establishes a pattern of violating traffic laws such as taking illegal left-hand turns or running red lights when no traffic is coming opens additional surveillance detection options. Such driving habits also serve the purposes of antisurveillance, which we will address in Chapter 12.

At the other extreme is slow and conservative driving. The Principal who drives in this manner inherits some surveillance detection advantages as well. Here too, if the Principal drives in a slow and conservative manner, the surveillance team is forced to conform to this pattern as well. If the Principal drives 5 miles per hour below the speed limit, he may upset a number of other vehicles, but he can easily isolate following vehicles that are maneuvering in a similar manner.

Driving patterns are used for detection purposes because a surveillance team will attempt to maintain mobile observation of the Principal from the rear. This requires that at least one surveillance vehicle maintain a following distance that is within observation range of the Principal but still provides a degree of security from detection. In most cases this will be dictated by the terrain and traffic obstacles. In open terrain such as on highways or rural state roads, a surveillance vehicle can increase the following distance because there is a greater observation range for both the surveillance vehicle and the Principal who may be observing to the rear. In denser city traffic the surveillance vehicle will normally have to follow more closely for observation and to ensure that traffic or traffic signals do not obstruct it from remaining with the Principal. Whatever the circumstances may be, the following surveillance vehicle will normally travel at a pace that is similar to the Principal's in order to maintain a standard secure following distance.

The Principal will use these factors for detection purposes. By gradually fluctuating from faster to slower speeds and vice versa, the Principal can observe for vehicles that mirror this driving pattern. If done gradually, this detection tactic should go unnoticed by the surveillance vehicle.

The brake lights of the Principal vehicle can be modified to facilitate this and other surveillance detection maneuvers. By installing a button that, when depressed, disengages the brake lights, the Principal can decrease vehicle speed without displaying the overt indicator of brake lights. The system should be installed so that the Principal must manually depress the disengage button the entire time it is in use. This prevents the Principal from accidentally leaving the system engaged, thus creating a suspicious appearance and a safety hazard. In employing this system, the Principal must ensure that his slowing activity is not so extreme that the malfunction is detectable by a surveillance team. Such a system is particularly effective at night, when it is more difficult to judge distance, possibly causing a surveillance vehicle to inadvertently close distance and then decrease speed in an unnatural manner. Manual transmission vehicles can decrease speed by downshifting rather than braking and projecting the brake lights.

More overt variations in speed can be employed on favorable terrain. In areas where there are bends in the road that would force a following surveillance vehicle to lose sight of the Principal temporarily, the Principal can travel at a faster speed going into the bend and then decrease his speed when completing it. If successful, this will result in a surveillance vehicle pursuing quickly around the bend and then bearing down on the slower-moving Principal when completing it. This will force the surveillance vehicle to either decrease its speed in an unnatural manner or pass the Principal. A poorly disciplined surveillance vehicle may even decrease its speed to reestablish a secure following distance, which will be very indicative of surveillance to the observant Principal. This tactic can also be used as the Principal passes over the crest of a hill and temporarily out of sight of a following surveillance vehicle.

Probably the most effective vehicular surveillance detection maneuver is the logical 180-degree turn. Note the term logical, implying that the circumstances of the turn should appear plausible to an observing surveillance team, if present. An example involves intersections at which it is difficult to execute a left turn due to heavy oncoming traffic or other obstacles. A logical maneuver to overcome this obstacle is for the Principal to continue straight until there is an opportunity to make a U-turn and return to turn right into the location. In some circumstances, such as when there is a median that obstructs a left turn, such a maneuver may be necessary and completely plausible. In any case, the 180-degree turn should be planned so that it there is a plausible conclusion to justify the maneuver.

The objectives of a logical 180-degree turn are to provide the Principal with an opportunity to observe following vehicles head-on and to elicit suspicious reactions from surveillance vehicles. When a surveillance team encounters a U-turn by the Principal, it should react in a standard manner. After observing the U-turn, or being informed of the maneuver by the command surveillance vehicle, any surveillance vehicles that can do so will attempt to pull off the road prior to the Principal's doubling back and passing them head-on. Surveillance vehicles that are able to pull off onto adjacent roads or into parking lots will immediately establish box positions to pick up the Principal and continue the follow as he passes back by.

Since the most effective pick-up positions will be established from the right side of the road in the Principal's direction of travel, surveillance vehicles will attempt to turn off the road to the left in reaction to the U-turn. The next standard reaction is for vehicles that are unable to turn off prior to being forced past the Principal to turn off the road at the first possible opportunity in order to circle back and rejoin the follow. Only a poorly disciplined surveillance vehicle would execute a U-turn to rejoin the follow. Figure 11 depicts the standard reaction of surveillance vehicles (S) to a U-turn by the Principal (P).

After executing the U-turn, the Principal will observe forward to get a good look at oncoming vehicles for retention or recognition. While doing so, he will also observe for any vehicles that appear to turn off the road in a hasty manner. If any vehicles are observed reacting in this manner, the Principal will observe for that particular vehicle where it turned off the road. The purpose of this is to determine whether the vehicle continued through the turn in a natural manner. Under such circumstances,

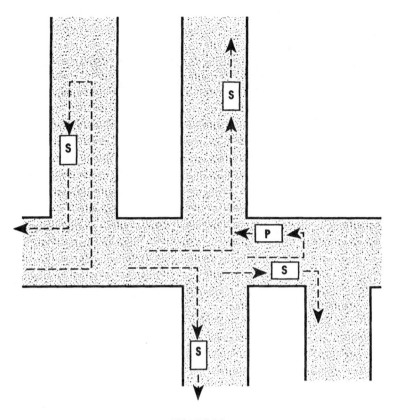

FIGURE 11

The standard reaction of surveillance vehicles to a U-turn by the Principal.

the Principal may be able to observe the vehicle turning to position itself to rejoin the follow. During the course of this maneuver, the Principal will also observe to the rear to identify any vehicles that turn off the road after passing by.

The Principal should plan a 180-degree turn based on the desired results. For example, if he is primarily concerned with observing following vehicles, he will execute the maneuver in a channelized location that provides no roads or parking lots for following traffic to turn into—forcing all following traffic to cross his path. This method is effective in providing a good look at all following vehicles, but it does little more in the way of surveillance detection unless a surveillance vehicle displays poor tactical discipline. When the Principal wants to observe how specific vehicles react to the 180-degree turn, he must do it in a location that provides options for surveillance vehicles to react, such as side streets to turn onto.

An overt but effective variation of the 180-degree turn is to combine it with a blind turn or crest. This may require that the Principal accelerate into the turn to ensure that any possible surveillance vehicles temporarily lose sight of him. When he executes a 180-degree turn within sight of the command surveillance vehicle, that vehicle has ample opportunity to inform the team and provide operators with more time to react. The command vehicle is caught completely off guard when it rounds a turn and is confronted with the Principal, who has executed a 180-degree turn.

This enhances the possibility of an unnatural reaction on the part of the command vehicle and may also deter it from informing the team of the maneuver until it has passed the Principal, so as to avoid appearing suspicious within observation range of the Principal. This, in turn, increases the possibility of other surveillance vehicles being unprepared and reacting unnaturally. It may also enable the Principal to observe indications that the surveillance vehicle navigator is transmitting immediate information to the team.

There are a number of active surveillance detection maneuvers that can be employed on the highway. Highways are normally favorable for surveillance detection because they are generally open and provide good fields of observation. Also, due to the fast rates of speed on highways, surveillance vehicles have little time to react to surveillance detection maneuvers.

One terrain feature that facilitates surveillance detection on highways is a rest area or a similar location such as a state welcome area or highway-side service station. As the Principal exits the highway and enters a rest area, he will observe to the rear for any vehicles that enter behind him. He can then take a position in the rest area to observe any vehicles that enter shortly after him. He will also observe the reactions of vehicles as he departs the area.

A more overt variation of this tactic is for the Principal to continue slowly through the rest area and reenter the highway, observing for any vehicle that entered behind him and does the same thing. This maneuver can be employed in another way as well. If a suspected surveillance vehicle has other vehicles in support, it will continue past the rest area when the Principal enters to allow a vehicle that is in a more discreet position to enter behind the Principal. As the Principal slowly travels through the rest area, he will observe the suspected surveillance vehicle as it passes by on the highway. He will then reenter the highway behind the suspected surveillance vehicle, at a nonintimidating distance, for observation purposes. If the vehicle is in fact a surveillance asset, it will likely exit the highway at the earliest possible opportunity to avoid additional exposure.

Another surveillance detection maneuver involving highway travel is for the Principal to simply exit the highway and observe for vehicles that exit behind him. This is particularly effective if employed immediately after passing a vehicle and then shifting right across both lanes of traffic to exit the highway. The act of passing another vehicle just prior to the exit provides a plausible reason for the abrupt maneuver. The primary objective of this maneuver is to isolate any vehicle that also shifts from the passing lane to exit the highway behind the Principal. Although any abrupt exit from the highway can be effective in isolating vehicles that also exit suddenly, it may be identified as an overt surveillance detection maneuver if there is no plausible reason to justify the action.

An overt variation of this maneuver can be executed on long highway exit lanes that allow vehicles to enter up to the point of the exit ramp. If the Principal decreases his speed and enters the exit lane at the earliest possible point, surveillance vehicles will have the opportunity to enter the exit lane prior to his actually reaching the exit ramp. Just before reaching the exit ramp, the Principal will shift back onto the highway and observe for any vehicles that mirror this action (see fig. 12).

Anytime the Principal wants to observe the vehicles that are traveling behind him on the highway, he can simply pull over into the breakdown lane and stop. This is a particularly overt maneuver, but it is effective in allowing the Principal to observe following vehicles as they pass. When he conducts this maneuver within observation range of a highway exit, the Principal should focus on vehicles that leave the highway at that exit, which would be the standard reaction of a surveillance vehicle. A varia-

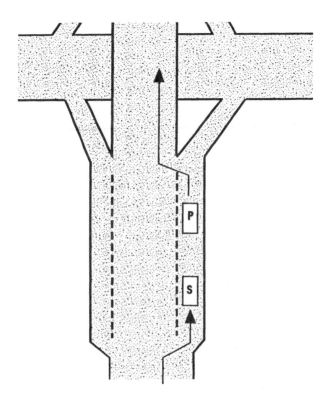

FIGURE 12

A long exit lane allows the Principal to enter early, wait for surveillance vehicles to enter, and, just before he reaches the exit ramp, shift back onto the highway. He can then watch for any vehicles that follow this erratic movement.

tion of this tactic is to pull over into the breakdown lane after entering a highway exit ramp. This extremely overt maneuver is effective in isolating, for observation purposes, vehicles that exit the highway behind the Principal. It is particularly effective when the characteristics of the exit ramp obstruct the view of following vehicles so that they do not realize the Principal has stopped until they are already committed to exiting the highway.

Another option when using highway exit ramps for surveillance detection is to continue straight through the exit and back onto the highway traveling in the same direction. A poorly disciplined surveillance vehicle may continue straight through as well. This maneuver is also effective in that a surveillance vehicle with adequate back-up will continue past the exit, allowing the Principal to reenter the highway from behind for observation purposes.

A variation of this technique can be very effective at complicated highway interchanges, the most basic of which is the cloverleaf. Many major interchanges are characterized by nonstandard road networking due to the number of avenues involved. By studying such interchanges in advance, the Principal can enter the interchange and then circle around and reenter the highway in the same direction as he was previously traveling. A surveillance vehicle that relies more on following the Principal than reading the map may mirror this action without realizing until it is too late that the route is illogical.

A final option when using a highway exit ramp for detection is for the Principal to exit, pass over the highway, and then reenter traveling in the opposite direction. This is an interesting challenge to a surveillance team, because in order to cover the Principal in a tactically sound manner, the team will have to expose at least two and possibly three surveillance vehicles. If the team does not counter the maneuver in a tactically sound manner, or does not have the surveillance vehicles necessary to rotate positions securely, the Principal can easily identify any vehicle that duplicates the maneuver in part or completely. This is a somewhat plausible three-sides-of-a-box SDR.

Although we have addressed these tactics as they apply to highway travel, the principles involved can be applied to virtually any type of vehicular road travel. Variations can be conducted on any type of street in both city and rural areas. For example, the tactic of rolling through a rest area and reentering the highway can be executed in any number of city parking lots. The Principal can also make unexpected maneuvers along any road, or in any number of locations to observe the reactions of surrounding vehicles or to observe passing vehicles that are channelized by the terrain.

Turn-only lanes are very common on city streets. These can be used in the same manner as long exit lanes on the highway. The Principal enters the turn lane, giving any following surveillance vehicles an opportunity to follow behind. Prior to making the mandatory turn, the Principal will reenter the main thoroughfare and observe for any vehicles that also shift out. This may be even more effective if the Principal engages his turn signal early into the maneuver, inducing a following surveillance vehicle to engage its signal, thus making any subsequent mirroring of the Principal particularly suspicious. There are also any number of opportunities on city streets to shift quickly across traffic and make a turn while observing for any vehicles that mirror this action.

Through area knowledge the Principal should be aware of back-street shortcuts that can be used to avoid lengthy traffic lights. Although others may also be aware of such shortcuts, most people are patient and conservative enough to travel by the main streets through the traffic light. As the Principal maneuvers through back streets to avoid a traffic light, he should observe for other vehicles that take the same route. In the same way, cutting through a parking lot to avoid a traffic light may also expose a poorly disciplined surveillance vehicle.

Channelized terrain and choke points facilitate surveillance detection. Channelized terrain refers to limited routes of travel available to a following surveillance team. A surveillance team prefers to commit as few surveillance vehicles as possible to the actual route the Principal is traveling. It will attempt to do so by using parallel routes. This type of coverage gives the team more flexibility in reacting to turns the Principal makes and minimizes the number of surveillance vehicles that can be exposed to the Principal. Having as few vehicles as necessary following on the same route as the Principal also leaves fewer vehicles vulnerable to detection by maneuvers such as a sudden stop or a 180-degree turn.

The Principal can force the surveillance team to channelize its vehicles by traveling on routes such as rural roads and bridges over waterways with no paralleling avenues. Channelized terrain offers no adjacent roads for surveillance vehicles to escape onto to avoid passing the Principal and being exposed by surveillance detection maneuvers. Many of the previously addressed tactics demonstrated the channelizing of following vehicles on the highway for surveillance detection purposes. Off the highway, such channelizing renders the surveillance team vulnerable to detection through passive observation or active measures such as the sudden stop or 180-degree turn. It also leaves the team susceptible to having all of its vehicles delayed by a traffic obstacle while the Principal drives away.

Choke points are terrain features that cause traffic to concentrate in density. In such locations, surveillance vehicles may be forced in behind the Principal closer than would otherwise be appropriate while also slowing or stagnating their movement, thus making them more vulnerable to observation from the Principal. Common examples of choke points are construction zones, school zones, and dense city traffic. An overt detection tactic associated with the use of a choke point involves the Principal turning onto an unmarked dead-end road or cul-de-sac to observe for any vehicles that follow and then react in an unnatural manner.

Toll booths are choke points that are generally associated with highways. These provide unique opportunities for surveillance detection. As the Principal approaches a toll booth barrier, he should enter the longest line if traffic is backed up. He will then observe for any other vehicles that enter the longer line rather than a shorter one. Any vehicles meeting this profile will be isolated and observed as a possible surveillance vehicle.

When entering the line, the Principal will also observe the vehicles that pass by to enter a shorter line—which would be the tactically sound reaction of a surveillance vehicle concerned with security. If the Principal encounters no lines when reaching the toll booths, he should fabricate a reason to delay passing through, such as fumbling for money, to allow any surveillance vehicles to pass through other available booths ahead of him. In this case, the Principal should observe the other vehicles to facilitate subsequent recognition.

After passing through the toll booth, the Principal will observe for vehicles that pull out behind him from subsequent interchanges, rest areas, and so forth, to determine whether they were among those that passed by at the toll booths.

When there is no restriction from channelized terrain, a surveillance team is able to execute a more secure follow. One tactic used to enhance security in a multiple-vehicle surveillance is for the command vehicle to continue straight at an intersection when the Principal turns. Then a surveillance vehicle that was not within observation range of the Principal prior to the turn will turn behind him in a secure manner to establish command. This tactic prevents the vulnerability to detection that exists anytime a surveillance vehicle within observation range of the Principal takes a turn behind him.

The most common and logical subsequent maneuver by the surveillance vehicle that continued straight is to continue to the next possible intersection and turn in a direction to parallel the Principal in order to continue in support of the surveillance operation. Given this understanding, when the Principal observes that a suspected surveillance vehicle has continued straight after he has turned, at the first possible opportunity, he will turn in the direction of the route a surveillance vehicle would use as a subsequent parallel. This tactic is designed to detect the suspected vehicle traveling on the paralleling route, which would be highly indicative of surveillance. Figure 13 depicts an example of this active surveillance detection maneuver.

When the Principal stops during the course of his travels, the surveillance team is forced to establish a box, similar to the stakeout box, to position vehicles along each route on which he might resume travel. These positions will be prioritized based on the likelihood of his selecting them. Surveillance vehicles will attempt to position themselves at the first possible location away from the Principal's stop point, in order to minimize the avenues onto which he can travel undetected before he reaches the location of the boxing surveillance vehicle. When the Principal stops, he should determine which routes the surveillance team would box for the pick-up. If there are locations that meet the profile of a box position, he can travel to them in an effort to identify a boxing surveillance vehicle. Figure 14 depicts one example of this concept.

Notice that each of the surveillance vehicles (S) are located in pick-up box positions along one of the Principal's (P) two initial routes of departure. Since it is assumed that the Principal will depart along the major route, the surveillance vehicles are positioned along the first secondary road to observe him pass by and then pull out to pursue. Recognizing this as a likely box position location, the Principal turns onto the secondary road, thus exposing the surveillance vehicle. This tactic is significantly enhanced when the Principal actually observes a suspected surveillance vehicle turning into a road, parking lot, or other location that might serve as a box position as he stops. By then

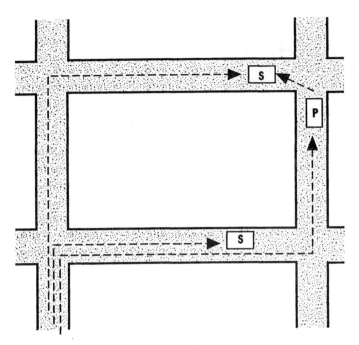

FIGURE 13

In this example, the Principal detects the surveillance vehicle that continued straight after he turned by turning immediately in the direction of the paralleling route which it would logically take in order to maintain command.

executing the maneuver depicted in Figure 14, he will effectively confirm surveillance if he detects the vehicle in a box position.

An overt variation of this tactic that the Principal can execute on a highway is to pull over in the breakdown lane prior to a rest area or similar location. After he stops, he will observe the following vehicles as they pass by. After a short delay, he will resume travel on the highway and pull into the rest area ahead. He will observe the vehicles inside the rest area to determine if any of them are among those which passed by on the highway. This is an effective maneuver because the rest area would be a logical location for a surveillance vehicle to establish a box position in reaction to the Principal's stop.

Another variation is to stop in the breakdown lane within observation range of the rest area. From this vantage point, the Principal can observe for any following vehicles that pass by and enter the rest area. He can then travel into the rest area to get a

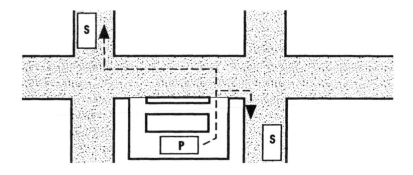

FIGURE 14

In this example, the Principal pulls into a gas station and surveillance vehicles establish a box by positioning themselves on each of the roads that intersect the major route closest to the stop. The Principal then drives to what he determines is a likely location of a box position and exposes one of the vehicles.

good look at the suspected surveillance vehicle for retention purposes. In this situation, he can create a plausible reason for the maneuver by checking under the hood as though experiencing mechanical problems.

Traveling by taxi does not preclude active surveillance detection. Passive observation is difficult because the Principal will not have the range of mirrors normally available. He has little to lose, however, by asking the taxi driver to observe for indications of surveillance. He simply tells the taxi driver that he suspects surveillance and that assistance in detection will be rewarded. Taxi drivers are generally good sources for observation because they are familiar with standard traffic patterns and can readily identify anything that appears suspicious. If the Principal is particularly concerned with the possibility of surveillance, he can instruct the taxi driver in surveillance detection maneuvers. This also provides a somewhat plausible reason for the use of overt tactics, because the surveillance team will likely attribute aggressive maneuvers to the erratic driving typical of cab drivers.

CHAPTER 9

ACTIVE FOOT SURVEILLANCE DETECTION

Active foot surveillance detection shares many of the principles of vehicular surveillance detection. As with passive foot surveillance detection, a primary disadvantage is the limited ability to discreetly observe to the rear. This disadvantage is offset, however, by terrain that is better suited to surveillance detection and the increased degree of flexibility with which the Principal can maneuver by foot. By vehicle the Principal is generally restricted to traveling on established roadways. By foot he can go virtually anywhere to conduct surveillance detection.

ACTIVE STAKEOUT DETECTION

The detection of foot stakeouts is limited primarily to the principles of passive surveillance addressed in Chapter 5. When it is possible for the Principal to travel by either foot or vehicle from a stakeout location, a surveillance team will place priority on positioning surveillance vehicles for a vehicular follow. This is because if the Principal departs the location by vehicle the surveillance team has less time to react and therefore must be prepared initially for a vehicular follow. If, however, the Principal departs the location by foot, surveillance operators will simply exit the surveillance vehicles and transition into a foot surveillance. The tactic addressed in the section on stakeout detection in Chapter 7, in which the

Principal departs the possible stakeout location by foot and walks through the area to identify surveillance assets, applies to foot surveillance stakeouts as well. The detection of a surveillance box that is established after the Principal stops during the course of a foot surveillance is limited primarily to the passive measures addressed in Chapter 5. This is due to the static and restricted nature of most stops, which considerably limits the number of active measures that can be employed to detect surveillance. The Principal should be particularly observant of individuals exiting vehicles as though to initiate a foot follow.

ACTIVE MOBILE SURVEILLANCE DETECTION

The Principal has few natural opportunities to observe for surveillance operators when traveling by foot on public streets and thoroughfares. Virtually the only ones are created when he increases his field of view by stopping, turning perpendicularly, or turning 180 degrees to change directions. The detection principles associated with the Principal making a turn and observing for possible surveillance operators were addressed in the section on passive foot surveillance detection in Chapter 5. Active surveillance detection tactics employed on public streets and thoroughfares are primarily associated with stops, perpendicular turns, and 180-degree turns, although others may be used as well.

One important note for this and all other foot surveillance detection maneuvers is that when observing possible surveillance operators at close range, the Principal should avoid making eye contact. Surveillance operators are generally paranoid about compromise, and eye contact with the Principal is viewed as an extreme degree of exposure. In many cases a surveillance operator will pull himself out of the operation if eye contact with the Principal occurs. This has a negative impact on the effectiveness of surveillance detection, because if the surveillance operator withdraws from the operation after the Principal gets a good look at him, the Principal loses the opportunity to observe him later and confirm surveillance. So observation for surveillance detection purposes should always be conducted in a discreet manner that will not cause surveillance operators to feel compromised.

Probably the oldest yet most effective method of foot surveillance detection is for the Principal to turn a blind corner and stop. Blind turns consist of intersections or other locations at which the Principal has the option to turn, causing any following surveillance operators to lose sight of him. Such locations are particularly characteristic of urban areas, where buildings line the sidewalk on virtually every block. The objective of this maneuver is to observe for possible surveillance operators after taking the blind turn and stopping. The Principal will focus on anyone who reacts in an unnatural manner when turning the corner and finding himself within exposure range of the Principal. Even a surveillance operator who maintains composure when confronted with such a situation will be exposed, thus facilitating future recognition by the Principal. Any stop made after a turn should be planned in advance and a plausible reason for it incorporated into the maneuver.

A well-coordinated surveillance team will approach any blind turn taken by the Principal with caution—being aware of the surveillance-detection implications. In such a situation, the surveillance team should commit a surveillance operator to continue straight at the location of the turn. This prevents his turning blindly into the Principal while still allowing him the opportunity to observe and determine whether the Principal has continued naturally through the turn. This operator will either inform the team that the corner is clear or that the Principal has stopped and that no operator should turn the corner. In either case, the surveillance operator must inform the team of the Principal's status. Based on this application, when stopping after a blind turn the Principal should observe for individuals who glance in his direction when passing through the location of the turn. The Principal should further observe for indications of the use of concealed body communications equipment or visual communications signals.

Through prior planning the Principal may incorporate entry of a public location into this maneuver. After he takes a blind turn he will immediately enter a public location, such as a store, which affords outside observation through a window. As he establishes a position from which to observe outside while conducting a natural activity, such as shopping, he will observe people who turn the corner. The Principal will focus on anyone who reacts suspiciously, meeting the profile of a perplexed surveillance operator who has lost his Principal. Such an individual may also begin scanning the area for locations where the Principal may have entered. Again, the Principal should observe for indications that an individual is communicating with others on the streets.

The logical 180-degree turn is executed on foot to achieve the same objectives as by vehicle. Here again, the Principal should incorporate a plausible reason for his action. When the Principal is traveling by foot, there is a lot of terrain that will facilitate this maneuver, particularly with prior planning. Again, the Principal should observe, for retention and recognition purposes, all individuals who had been following, as well as those who appear to maneuver out of his path to avoid detection.

A variation of the 180-degree turn is to cross the street at an intersection and then backtrack in the previous direction of travel on the opposite side of the street. Again, the Principal should incorporate a logical reason for backtracking, such as to enter a store. In this case it is feasible that the Principal simply went to a controlled intersection to cross the street instead of jaywalking. Following this logic, surveillance operators will generally expect the Principal to cross the street at intersections. For this reason they will establish an enhanced security posture as he approaches an intersection in anticipation of a possible turn. By crossing the street in the middle of the block, the Principal may catch surveillance operators in a vulnerable position and force a suspicious reaction. An overt variation of this maneuver is when the Principal follows it with a 180-degree turn as opposed to continuing in the direction he was traveling prior to his crossing.

Channelized Terrain and Choke Points

On foot, the Principal can use channelized terrain and choke points for the same objectives as were addressed in the last chapter with regard to active vehicular surveillance detection. Channelized terrain may consist of tunneled walkways, street overpasses, or waterway overpasses. The channelized terrain may facilitate rear observation, but normally it will also be exploited through the incorporation of a 180-degree turn or stop. Some channelized terrain may offer the Principal a natural opportunity to observe to the rear. An example of this is a bridge over a river.

Since such a terrain feature will provide surveillance operators with the only nearby location to cross the water obstacle with the Principal, they will have no other option but to commit surveillance operators onto the bridge behind him.

As the Principal reaches the crest or middle of the bridge, he will stop as though to enjoy the view. At this point he will have the opportunity to observe to the rear for possible surveillance operators. He should focus on anyone who also stops as though to enjoy the view rather than continuing toward him. At this point he may also choose to execute a 180-degree turn to further observe the reactions of suspicious individuals. It is plausible that the Principal simply entered the bridge to enjoy the view and return. This tactic is applicable to many types of channelized terrain.

The most common choke points available to the Principal for surveillance detection are public locations. Variations of the previously discussed tactic of entering a public location after a blind turn to observe outside for surveillance operators can be employed in any public location. As the Principal enters the public location he can observe outside for surveillance operators as they maneuver to box positions to make the pick-up when he exits. The Principal should select a secure position—such as a seat near the window in a restaurant, cafe, or bar—that offers good outside observation while appearing natural to surveillance operators who may enter behind him. The Principal will observe for individuals who pass the location in an unnatural manner or even pass by it more than once.

Public Locations

Public locations offer the best opportunities for foot surveillance detection. The basic principles of surveillance in public locations are similar to those of choke points addressed in the previous section, in that they force surveillance operators to concentrate and stagnate. The presence of restrictive boundaries and nonstandard terrain imposes unique restrictions and vulnerabilities on surveillance operators. In most cases, public locations will force surveillance operators closer to the Principal than they would otherwise allow themselves to get.

Public locations are characterized by nonstandard terrain because the possibilities are so varied, including department stores, malls, business complexes, and parks. The nonstandard terrain works to the benefit of the Principal for surveillance detection purposes because it forces the surveillance team to use special tactics. For example, a surveillance team can operate very effectively against a Principal on foot or by vehicle out on the streets, because it can employ its tactics systematically. In public locations, however, it must adapt its tactics to the specific circumstances encountered. This forces the team to rely more on resourcefulness than a systematic, planned formula of tactics, rendering it more vulnerable.

Public locations are also excellent for surveillance detection because they offer a number of opportunities for logical 180-degree turns. Consider the degree of unpredictability that the Principal can incorporate into his maneuvers in a mall or department store. While such locations provide excellent opportunities to observe surveillance operators if present, they can rarely serve to confirm surveillance unless an operator acts in a particularly suspicious manner. The reason for this is that it is not uncommon to observe the same individual any number of times when moving through such locations.

Public locations require surveillance operators to react immediately to a situation in a natural manner. When individuals go into a public location such as a store, they do so with a purpose. When surveillance operators go into a public location behind the Principal, they do so to observe the Principal. To do this in a natural manner, they must also contrive a plausible and natural reason for entering the location. This again forces them to be resourceful in maintaining an unsuspicious appearance. Remaining inconspicuous while observing a Principal in unfamiliar terrain is a difficult task for the surveillance operator. For this reason, the Principal should observe for people who appear out of place. In most cases this will be an almost instinctive assessment rather than a specific observation. One further consideration is that a public location with multiple exits will normally force a surveillance team to send in more operators because of the difficulty involved with the stakeout of multiple exits.

A way to force surveillance operators into a position that leaves them vulnerable to isolation is to enter a location they would be completely unprepared for in terms of dress or action.

By entering a location characterized by the unique dress of its clientele, the Principal can then observe for and isolate those whose clothing style does not conform. College bars, biker bars, and high-class restaurants are only a few such locations that a surveillance team may have difficulty reacting to in a quick and natural manner. If the surveillance team feels that the activity to be conducted inside the location is worthy of observation, it may commit operators inside who are not adequately dressed to blend with surrounding individuals. If his intent is to remain discreet, the Principal must select locations that will appear plausible to the surveillance team based on established patterns.

Another way to force surveillance operators into a situation they may be unprepared for is to enter a public location where a specific type of action is required to blend with the surroundings. This enables the Principal to isolate and observe individuals who are not comfortable with the required activity. One example of such a location is a pool hall. A surveillance operator cannot enter a pool hall behind the Principal and appear natural without actually playing pool. Perhaps the surveillance operator is comfortable with a pool cue, but it's just as likely that he will be among the least proficient players in the hall. By identifying individuals who appear to be novices at the activity required, the Principal can isolate possible operators. Again, the location should appear plausible to the surveillance team.

When entering a public location such as a restaurant for the purposes of surveillance detection, the Principal should position himself in a spot that provides a wide field of view of the other people inside. If possible, he should sit in an area that allows him to see the entrance and observe for anyone who enters after him, isolating those who enter after him as possible surveillance operators. He will focus on those who sit in a position that facilitates their observation of him and who enter and sit alone. An individual entering to join someone else who is sitting alone may also be an indicator of surveillance if the surveillance team has committed another operator into the restaurant to sit with the fellow operator in order to provide a more natural appearance.

An overt detection tactic employed in such a situation is for the Principal to sit in a restaurant long enough for any surveillance operators to enter and get positioned and then leave without ordering, as though he were not pleased with the menu selection. He will then establish a position outside of the restaurant to observe for individuals who also depart in this manner. A variation of this is for the Principal to order a meal that can be served and consumed quickly. Any surveillance operators in the restaurant will order a meal to appear natural. By leaving quickly, the Principal may catch them off guard and in the middle of a meal. He will then observe to see if any of the restaurant's other patrons end their meals quickly and depart behind him.

The Principal can use very small and confined public locations as choke points to force surveillance operators close in for observation. A surveillance team, however, will rarely commit surveillance operators into an extremely confined public location unless the expected benefit outweighs the consequences of exposing the operators to the Principal. Moderately sized public locations, such as shops and convenience stores, provide excellent surveillance detection opportunities. The location selected should be one that has sufficient space to give surveillance operators enough of a sense of security that they will enter behind the Principal but that is small enough to allow the Principal to observe everyone inside with relative ease.

As the Principal enters the location, he should travel to the rear while observing those who were there before him. He will eliminate these people as possible surveillance operators. After he is satisfied that he has identified all of the individuals who were there prior to his entry, he will gradually move toward the front in a natural manner. This allows him to isolate all those who entered after him. He will observe these individuals for retention or recognition and to identify whether they display any other indicators of surveillance, such as appearing unnatural in the surroundings. Single-entry/exit establishments are best for use with this tactic because they limit the avenues by which individuals can enter without observation by the Principal.

Such establishments are also conducive to surveillance detection because a single entrance serves to channelize surveillance operators through an effective detection point. Given appropriate cover, the Principal can enter such a location and establish a position that enables him to observe anyone else who enters. He will observe everyone for retention purposes and for indications of surveillance, such as immediately scanning the location as though searching for someone.

Many public locations have features such as elevators, escalators, and stairways that are characteristic of channelized terrain. Elevators are also similar to choke points in that they force surveillance operators close to the Principal. The Principal should be suspicious of anyone who enters an elevator with him and immediately selects the top level or perhaps even asks the Principal which level he would like, offering to push the button for him. Stairwells are effective in channelizing surveillance operators for obvious reasons. The design of most escalators not only provides the Principal with the opportunity to channelize possible surveillance operators but to execute two, sequential 180-degree turns as well. By approaching an escalator in the direction opposite that in which it moves, he naturally executes a 180-degree turn in order to get on, which allows him to observe following individuals in an inconspicuous manner. Upon getting off, he turns 180 degrees again, creating another natural opportunity to observe those who got on the escalator behind him.

Public Transportation

Chapter 5 addressed the passive detection measures involved with public transportation. Active measures employed in these circumstances build on opportunities that are initiated through passive means.

Recall that when traveling by bus, surveillance operators will attempt to sit as far to the rear as possible to enhance observation. To counter this, the Principal should sit as far to the rear of the bus as possible to observe individuals who board at subsequent stops. If a surveillance operator is already sitting to the rear as the Principal selects a seat in the same proximity, this will certainly make the operator uncomfortable and may make him act in an unnatural manner. If the Principal is already at the rear when a surveillance operator enters the bus, the operator will be forced to sit closer to the front to avoid getting too close to the Principal. As passengers enter the bus, the Principal should observe for anyone who begins moving toward the rear but stops suddenly to sit upon observing that the Principal is already in the rear.

One overt method of surveillance detection involving public buses is for the Principal to remain at a bus stop and not enter the bus as other individuals at the stop do. Obviously, anyone who does the same should be regarded as a possible surveillance operator. At stops that service multiple bus routes, the Principal must be aware of the various routes in order to determine which individuals have remained at the stop after all possible buses have passed.

Another overt method of surveillance detection involving bus travel is for the Principal to stay on the bus through the last stop and identify anyone who has also followed this illogical pattern. A surveillance operator who is not familiar with the bus route may be easily exposed by this tactic. To ensure the effectiveness of this tactic, the Principal must be familiar with the route and observe all individuals who enter the bus after him. This enables him to determine the point along the route at which a given individual's continued presence becomes illogical and suspicious.

Trains and passenger buses are fairly limited in the options they provide for discreet surveillance detection. As addressed in Chapter 5, a surveillance team may use train and bus travel as an opportunity to place a surveillance operator up against the Principal. Although the security-minded Principal should approach any such contact with caution, these circumstances also offer him the opportunity to provide a possible surveillance effort with deceptive or misleading information. The Principal's primary concern in such situations is to ensure that the surveillance team cannot invalidate the information he provides through previous observations or other means, thus disclosing his deceptive measures.

The well-documented Hollywood tactics of surveillance detection through the use of public transportation, primarily mass transit such as subways, are likely the most common to the novice. Tactics such as jumping off a subway train to detect a surveillance operator who mirrors this activity are neither effective against a sophisticated surveillance effort nor consistent with the principle of discretion. However, any Principal who meets the criteria of an overt target, as addressed in Chapter 2, can certainly use public transportation as an effective means of active surveillance detection. On any mode of public transportation he can do so by moving unexpectedly in a manner contrary to the natural flow of movement and identifying individuals who react to this.

ACTIVE FOOT SURVEILLANCE DETECTION AT NIGHT

Limited visibility at night generally dictates that surveillance operators follow in a manner that minimizes the possibility of losing sight of the Principal even momentarily. The principles of darkness adaptation and observation are applied most effectively against a target object. This means that night observation techniques such as scanning and off-center viewing are much more effective for observing an already identified object than for finding an object in darkness. A surveillance operator who is proficient in the principles of darkness adaptation and observation will understand the importance of maintaining constant command at night. This generally dictates a tighter method of coverage. Additionally, the enhanced concealment provided by darkness may give a following foot surveillance operator an increased sense of security.

The enhanced degree of concealment and decreased visual acuity are factors the Principal will exploit in conducting active surveillance detection at night. Distance perception is degraded at night, which enables the Principal to fluctuate his speed in order to bring a surveillance operator closer or force him to hasten his pace. A significant increase in speed has the same effect as accelerating into a blind turn. To maintain or reestablish observation in darkness, a surveillance operator may bear down on the Principal blindly and react in a suspicious manner when he finds himself uncomfortably close. Additionally, the more aggressive pace of a surveillance operator attempting to close distance on the Principal may be audibly detectable.

Recall that blind turns are used in active surveillance detection. At night, the Principal can use the characteristics of darkness to employ the concepts of a blind turn in many more locations, so the tactic becomes much more flexible. Surveillance operators may react more aggressively to any circumstance of lost visibility at night, due to previously addressed factors. The number of specific examples in which the Principal can use darkness to drastically decrease his rate of speed or stop in a location that is undetectable to surveillance operator is unlimited. Recall that hearing and smell are enhanced senses of observation at night.

CHAPTER 10

COUNTER-SURVEILLANCE

Countersurveillance differs significantly from other methods of physical surveillance detection in that it consists of actions taken by a third party—consisting of one or more persons—to detect the presence of surveillance on the Principal. The term third party simply separates countersurveillance operators from the first person (the Principal) and the secondary surveillance operators. The Principal may use trusted associates as third parties to provide countersurveillance coverage. Due to the expertise and discipline required, it is best to employ professional surveillance operators from private investigative agencies or other organizations that maintain a capable surveillance team.

Countersurveillance is the most sophisticated and effective method of physical surveillance detection. All methods of surveillance detection addressed to this point involve the Principal observing his surroundings to identify the presence of surveillance. Countersurveillance allows the Principal to travel in a more natural manner since he does not have to concentrate on observing for surveillance coverage. And countersurveillance assets are able to position themselves in locations that will provide a field of observation the Principal would not be able to achieve himself. Countersurveillance will normally be employed as a final confirmation measure after the

Principal has found specific indicators of surveillance through other detection measures.

Countersurveillance is very characteristic of intelligence and law enforcement agency activities. When intelligence operatives meet with their agents, they commonly employ the support of countersurveillance to ensure that their activities are not compromised or that their contact is not a double-agent. Intelligence agencies will also employ countersurveillance when they suspect that an agent is under surveillance. If surveillance is detected during countersurveillance coverage, the agency will confirm that the agent is compromised and either discontinue contact or incorporate more secure means of contact and control. Law enforcement agencies commonly employ countersurveillance to ensure the security of their agents during undercover operations such as narcotics buys.

COUNTERSURVEILLANCE PLANNING

As with all methods of surveillance detection, countersurveillance should be conducted in a systematic manner based on target pattern analysis. Countersurveillance requires more thorough planning because the Principal must synchronize his travel and movements with the countersurveillance coverage. The countersurveillance plan may comprise nothing more than observing the Principal's standard travels, or it may incorporate surveillance detection maneuvers as addressed in the previous chapters.

Countersurveillance is most effectively employed at designated locations that are suitable for the isolation and identification of surveillance operators. This enables countersurveillance operators to establish static positions with appropriate cover, concealment, and observation. Countersurveillance coverage that moves with the Principal is much less effective and also makes countersurveillance operators vulnerable to detection by the surveillance team.

The countersurveillance plan will normally be developed around a surveillance detection route. The SDR developed for countersurveillance will differ from that used in surveillance detection because it will normally be established around surveillance detection points (SDP), which are designated locations where countersurveillance operators can isolate and detect surveillance coverage. An effective SDR will incorporate at least five SDPs. Recall that surveillance operators are most vulnerable to detection when they are forced into confined or static positions that provide limited cover. SDPs give countersurveillance operators opportunities to exploit these vulnerabilities.

The SDR developed for countersurveillance must appear logical to a surveillance team, if present, but not be logical for others to travel along the same route. To facilitate this, the SDR will normally have a theme. As an example, the Principal might travel to any number of hardware stores as though shopping for or pricing particular items. This establishes a logical reason for traveling an otherwise illogical route, while providing SDPs (the hardware stores themselves) for countersurveillance operators to concentrate on. Any individual other than the Principal who is observed at two or more of these locations will indicate surveillance coverage.

The resources necessary to conduct countersurveillance can be extensive or very minimal. Although it may seem as though manning up to five separate SDPs would be manpower-intensive, this is not necessarily the case. In fact, it is preferable that the same countersurveillance operator or operators rotate to each SDP, because this makes it easier to confirm surveillance by negating the guesswork involved with comparing descriptions of the possible surveillance operators observed by different countersurveillance operators. If different countersurveillance operators are employed at separate SDPs, they should take photographs of possible surveillance operators when practical. Composite drawings will also assist in comparing observed individuals.

Another disadvantage in having different countersurveillance operators man separate SDPs is that it is often difficult to isolate possible surveillance operators at a single location. A well-trained and disciplined surveillance team can operate with a level of proficiency that will make it difficult for even a concentrated countersurveillance effort to detect operators at a given location. When the same countersurveillance operators man each SDP, they can virtually confirm surveillance by observing the same individual a number of times in unrelated locations. This is much more conclusive than relying upon the detection of isolated incidents that are indicative of surveillance.

The difficulty involved in moving countersurveillance operators to the various SDPs is easily overcome through thorough planning. As we will discuss later, it is essential that countersurveillance operators be positioned at SDPs prior to the Principal's arrival. To facilitate this, the SDR can incorporate actions that give countersurveillance operators time to reposition. Another option is to develop a plan wherein countersurveillance operators depart the SDP before the Principal does. This can be coordinated by timing, specified activities of the Principal, or a discreet signal provided by the Principal.

A primary concern for any countersurveillance operation is security. A surveillance team's detection of countersurveillance involves the same consequences associated with its identification of any surveillance detection practice. With the exception of the coordination required to move the same countersurveillance operators between separate SDPs, the only disadvantage to this method of manning SDPs is the operators' inherent vulnerability to detection. Just as the objective of the countersurveillance coverage is to identify the same individuals at separate, unrelated locations, surveillance operators will certainly confirm surveillance detection when they identify countersurveillance operators at these incoincidental locations.

Prior to any countersurveillance operation, countersurveillance operators must conduct reconnaissance of proposed SDPs. The Principal should not be involved in this because of the obvious threat of actual surveillance—which would result in an equally obvious compromise—at this point. The reconnaissance should evaluate possible SDPs for cover, concealment, and observation. An understanding of how a surveillance team will operate in a specific situation should provide the basis for the positioning of countersurveillance operators in order to maximize the probability of surveillance detection. The need to establish well-concealed countersurveillance locations applies during all countersurveillance activities, but it is significantly greater when employing the same operators at separate SDPs. This concealment must be achieved while still establishing an effective observation position. In planning for countersurveillance operations, each SDP must be evaluated to ensure that it satisfies these criteria.

As is the case with surveillance operators, countersurveillance operators must determine the cover for actions that they will take during the operation. This cover should be determined based on the worst-case assumption that the countersurveillance operator will undergo the scrutiny of surveillance operators. Even when a countersurveillance position is identified as offering a unique degree of concealment that deems the probability of compromise low, countersurveillance operators must still maintain effective cover for action to avoid arousing the suspicions of other individuals who may take actions that compromise the operation.

In formalizing the countersurveillance plan, countersurveillance operators will inform the Principal of where they will be located at each SDP so that he will avoid moving too close in or having an unplanned contact with one of them. Given this information, the Principal must practice discipline in overcoming the natural tendency to look in their direction during the operation.

When the plan involves the same countersurveillance operators manning multiple SDPs, a plan for their disguise is also required. A professional surveillance team is well practiced in the principles of observation and operates under the assumption that countersurveillance coverage is always possible. If at any point during the course of a countersurveillance operation an operator assesses that there is the slightest possibility of scrutiny from a surveillance operator, he must execute an appearance change prior to continuing in the operation.

The principles of disguise addressed in Chapter 4 apply to countersurveillance operators as well. In most cases, it is more effective for a countersurveillance operator to use a disguise at the beginning of the operation, because it is easier and faster to take off a disguise than to apply one. When necessary, a countersurveillance operator should forgo the coverage of an SDP in order to take the time to apply an effective disguise.

If at any point in the countersurveillance operation an operator believes that he may have been observed, even in the slightest, by a surveillance operator, he must determine the feasibility of continuing. This should be based on whether he can employ a disguise or man positions at subsequent SDPs that will ensure with absolute certainty that he will not be detected. If he has any doubt, he should terminate his involvement in the operation. The countersurveillance plan must also incorporate emergency contact procedures or signals that a countersurveillance operator can use to instruct other operators to terminate the operation when he has assessed that the surveillance team may suspect countersurveillance.

Concealed body communications equipment assists coordination during a countersurveillance operation, but for security reasons, the Principal should not wear any such equipment. The countersurveillance plan may include discreet signals from the Principal to countersurveillance operators, to inform them to move to the next SDP or terminate the operation, for instance. Any signal employed should be a natural action that would not draw the suspicion of surveillance operators. It should not be a quick movement such as scratching the head or checking the watch, because countersurveillance operators' attention will be focused primarily on activities taking place around the Principal, and only periodically on the Principal himself. Any signals used should be longer-term, such as placing a newspaper under the arm or purchasing a drink.

Countersurveillance operators should rarely be required to signal the Principal during the course of an operation. In fact, requiring the Principal to observe a countersurveillance operator in order to receive a signal is an extremely poor security practice, as it may direct surveillance operators' attention to the countersurveillance operators and compromise the operation.

There are unique situations in which the nature of the surveillance threat or the purpose of the countersurveillance operation dictates that the Principal be informed at the first indication of surveillance. An example might be when the Principal is concerned with the possibility of an attack or when the purpose of countersurveillance coverage is to ensure that surveillance is not present in order to allow the Principal to conduct protected activity. Under such circumstances, the plan should incorporate a signal that does not require direct interface between the Principal and countersurveillance operators, such as a beverage can placed in a specified location that the Principal will walk by.

THE COUNTERSURVEILLANCE OPERATION

The SDR for a countersurveillance operation should begin at a stakeout location. Recall that the stakeout is a phase in which a surveillance team is particularly vulnerable to detection because it must remain in static positions for extended periods of time. A team may tend to be less vigilant in its security measures when it is certain that the Principal is inside the stakeout location. This facilitates discreet countersurveillance observation of the possible stakeout area to detect surveillance operators or vehicles.

Given an understanding of how a surveillance team transitions from the stakeout phase into the pick-up and follow, countersurveillance operators will observe for these indicators as the Principal departs the stakeout location. They will position themselves based on the Principal's preplanned direction of travel from the stakeout location. In this application, countersurveillance can be very effective in identifying vehicles or individuals moving from a static to mobile status as the Principal departs the stakeout location and noting them as possible surveillance assets.

Recall that there should be no mobile countersurveillance coverage during the mobile phase of the operation due to the security risks of countersurveillance operators mirroring the Principal's travels. A primary rule for the manning of SDPs is that countersurveillance operators must be in position at the SDP before the Principal arrives. One reason for this is that it gives them an opportunity to establish their positions with cover and concealment before the surveillance effort arrives, precluding the possibility of observation by surveillance operators who arrive with the Principal.

Although SDPs will normally involve a static location for the reasons previously addressed, in some circumstances terrain may facilitate the positioning of an SDP along a mobile portion of the SDR. Recall that channelized terrain and choke points are very effective in making surveillance assets vulnerable to detection. This applies to an even greater degree to countersurveillance operations, due to the enhanced observation and detection capability involved. Countersurveillance operators will man static positions along a route where they can exploit these surveillance vulnerabilities.

When SDPs are positioned along mobile routes, the terrain must provide adequate concealment to countersurveillance operators and restrict the rate of movement through the area so that countersurveillance operators have time to observe and note all following foot and vehicular traffic. One example of exploiting channelized terrain in a secure manner is the use of pedestrian overpasses. Countersurveillance operators can establish a secure position from which to observe for individuals who enter the overpass after the Principal. This provides an opportunity to use vision enhancement devices or to videotape all those passing through the channelized terrain. In this particular example, countersurveillance operators should also observe individuals who opt not to use the overpass and instead cross the street in an unconventional manner.

Operational effectiveness is the primary reason for countersurveillance operators to man their SDP positions prior to the Principal's arrival. All SDPs will require that the surveillance team transition from a mobile follow to a surveillance box, similar to a stakeout box. Some will require that the surveillance team transition from a vehicular follow to a foot follow and then to a surveillance box. It is during all such transitions that a surveillance team is particularly vulnerable to detection, because they are periods of anxious uncertainty for the team. During such transitions, the surveillance team may compromise secure tactical discipline and execution to ensure that it maintains command of the Principal. So when countersurveillance coverage is in place at the SDP to observe the area during these transition periods, the surveillance team is particularly vulnerable to detection.

One thing of note that makes surveillance operators particularly vulnerable to countersurveillance coverage is their communications practices. A disciplined surveillance operator will rarely transmit information via concealed body communications equipment when it might be detectable by the Principal, because there is little information he should need to transmit during the course of a surveillance operation that cannot wait until he is certain his actions are secure. However, given scrutiny, the use of concealed body communications equipment will still be readily detectable by the trained observer. Compounding this vulnerability is the fact that surveillance operators tend to be more careless in transmitting information when they are certain their actions are undetectable by the Principal.

A surveillance team's use of visual communications signals is particularly vulnerable to countersurveillance. Countersurveillance operators should have a field of observation that will enable them to observe how signals are used and how the surveillance team interacts. All such surveillance team communications, while rarely observable by the Principal himself, are vulnerabilities that countersurveillance can capitalize on.

Recall that public locations are effective in drawing surveillance operators into a confining area that is suitable for surveillance detection. Public locations are equally effective for countersurveillance, provided that countersurveillance operators can ensure an appropriate degree of cover and concealment. Incorporating a public location as an SDP can be a very effective surveillance detection measure, as it forces surveillance operators into unfamiliar terrain that offers only limited options for developing cover for action. Public locations with only one entrance can be used effectively as SDPs, as they channelize all following individuals through a single point, allowing for the observation of possible surveillance operators.

The number of public locations that are suitable for countersurveillance is unlimited. A restaurant is an example of one that is particularly effective. Countersurveillance coverage of a Principal dining in a restaurant provides a degree of observation that is absolutely impossible for a lone Principal to achieve. Countersurveillance operators can observe as individual patrons enter the establishment and coordinate their seating arrangements, noting those who appear interested in the activities of the Principal while dining.

An effective tactic that can be incorporated into the countersurveillance plan involving a restaurant is to set up a dinner meeting between the Principal and another individual. In such a situation, a surveillance team will be particularly interested in placing an operator in a location that will facilitate overhearing any conversation between the two. This offers unique opportunities for countersurveillance operators to observe how other patrons react to the activities of the Principal. Of particular value to surveillance detection effort is the reaction of surrounding individuals as the Principal departs the restaurant. Countersurveillance operators will observe for individuals who display particular interest, appear to communicate by a concealed communications means, or move to make a phone call. They should remain in the restaurant after the Principal has departed to observe for individuals who conclude their meals unnaturally and leave.

It may be necessary for countersurveillance operators to depart a SDP before the Principal in order to ensure that they are positioned at the next SDP prior to his arrival. A disadvantage of this is that it precludes their observing for surveillance as the Principal transitions from a static to mobile portion of the SDR. When possible, the SDR should be developed so as to allow countersurveillance operators time to observe this transition and still move to the next SDP ahead of the Principal. This can be arranged by the Principal taking a longer yet still logical route or making a short stop, such as for gasoline, along the way to the SDP.

COUNTERSURVEILLANCE TO SURVEILLANCE TRANSITION

An extension of countersurveillance coverage that is extremely sophisticated and complex involves employing countersurveillance to isolate a suspected surveillance operator and then following that individual to confirm surveillance and determine his identity. This is an aggressive measure to detect surveillance at its source. Obviously, it requires that countersurveillance operators be tactically capable surveillance operators as well.

Concealed communications equipment significantly enhances the effectiveness of such operations, because it enables countersurveillance operators to coordinate the transition from the countersurveillance operation to a surveillance operation efficiently. It also enables foot countersurveillance operators to coordinate with a vehicular support team when the target transitions to a vehicle. When communications equipment is not available, the countersurveillance team must incorporate a visual signaling system that enables a countersurveillance operator to initiate the follow while other operators join in. When this is initiated, the actions of the lead operator should make the target of the surveillance obvious to the other operators. At this point, the operation will proceed as a standard foot surveillance follow.

To facilitate the effectiveness of the operation, a discreet signal should be provided to the Principal, as previously detailed, to inform him to proceed directly to a controlled location such as his residence. This enables the operators to cut to the chase without the distractors involved in following the remaining portions of the SDR. At this point the objective of the operation is to determine the identity of the target individual or at least to observe activities that will confirm surveillance beyond a doubt.

Without communications equipment it is extremely difficult to coordinate a follow with a vehicular support team. In this situation, the operation will normally be limited to following the target to a vehicle that he will drive or one that picks him up. In either case, the operators must note the license plate of the vehicle in order to satisfy the objective of the operation. During this period, the operators should be able to identify specific indicators of surveillance tactics if the target is in fact a surveillance operator. Actions other than traveling away from the SDP as the Principal departs will indicate that he is not a surveillance operator or that he has detected the countersurveillance activities.

The most comprehensive countersurveillance operation for detecting surveillance at its source will incorporate vehicular surveillance, enabling the countersurveillance team to follow the target individual away from the SDP. This practice is most effective when the countersurveillance team uses communications equipment to coordinate the pick-up of the vehicle the target enters. Anyone who is actually a member of a surveillance team will move in the direction of the Principal. Even when operating against a disciplined surveillance team, countersurveillance operators will observe activities that are indicative of surveillance. For example, if the target continues straight at an intersection when the Principal turns, its subsequent actions of will disclose whether it is a surveillance asset. After relinquishing command of the Principal to another surveillance asset, the target will turn at the next available opportunity and continue in support of the surveillance operation, unless countersurveillance is suspected.

As previously addressed, if the Principal departs a SDP by

vehicle, the target—if in fact he is a surveillance operator continuing in the operation—will also depart by vehicle, either as a driver or a passenger. The countersurveillance team will at least identify the vehicle if it is unable to follow due to resource constraints or if it loses the vehicle during the subsequent follow. Ideally, the countersurveillance team will follow the target to the Principal's destination, but when this is not possible, it should expect to observe that vehicle in the vicinity of the Principal's destination. When necessary, the countersurveillance team will maneuver to the Principal's location and actively search for that vehicle in the vicinity.

After either following a vehicle to the Principal's location or detecting the previously identified vehicle there, the countersurveillance team will establish a surveillance box around it. The team should establish a secure way to contact the Principal and instruct him to remain indefinitely until the surveillance vehicle departs. In selecting the method of communication, the team should consider the possibility of technical monitoring of the Principal's location. As the surveillance vehicle departs, the countersurveillance team will follow it in order to develop further identifying information.

CHAPTER 11

TECHNICAL SURVEILLANCE DETECTION

Conducting technical surveillance requires extensive technical expertise. The intent of this chapter is not to detail all aspects of a sophisticated technical inspection, but rather to provide an overview of general practical methods that can be employed at the novice level.

Technical surveillance detection detects the use of technical devices or equipment for surveillance and monitoring. This discipline is most commonly referred to as technical surveillance countermeasures (TSCM). Technical surveillance devices can be detected by conducting a physical search or using technical detection equipment. Any activities conducted to detect the presence of technical surveillance capabilities must be performed discreetly and systematically.

There are several reasons for such discretion. The first is that, as with any form of surveillance detection, it is important that the Principal not alert the surveillance effort to his surveillance consciousness. Such a disclosure can only result in more cautious or sophisticated methods of technical surveillance coverage.

Discretion is paramount when using technical detection equipment. Many devices can be activated and deactivated remotely to monitor conversation or activity only at specified times. While this conserves power in battery-operated devices, its primary purpose is security. Technical devices generate a much greater electrical signature when operating, and radio frequency devices transmit a constant signal, making them particularly susceptible to detection when in use. Therefore, to limit the degree of vulnerability, technical devices will only be activated when needed. If a surveillance team suspects that a technical surveillance inspection is planned or ongoing, it will certainly disengage any technical surveillance devices, which would degrade the effectiveness of the inspection considerably.

Another reason for discretion is that a detected surveillance device left in place and active can be used against an unwitting surveillance effort. If the Principal avoids alerting the surveillance effort, he can use the device to feed the team misleading or deceptive information.

Technical surveillance detection activities should not be discussed openly, particularly over a phone or in an area that may be the target of surveillance. Depending on the level of expertise required, professional inspectors may be needed to perform the technical surveillance detection activity because they will have the expensive equipment needed to conduct a thorough inspection. However, the Principal should be careful in determining the qualifications of the inspectors. Also, he should commission technical surveillance experts in a secure manner, including the use of physical antisurveillance when traveling to their offices. The discreet entry of technical surveillance inspectors into the target area should be planned and executed meticulously.

Technical surveillance detection requires a degree of expertise, but this does not preclude the Principal's undertaking measures to protect his own privacy and security. Much of the technical surveillance countermeasure equipment on the market is relatively easy to use, although expensive.

The search for technical surveillance devices can be divided into two phases—physical inspection and technical inspection. Even if the Principal does not have the equipment or professional services necessary to conduct the latter, it is still appropriate to conduct a physical search, because this is how about 90 percent of all technical surveillance equipment is detected.

PHYSICAL DETECTION

The physical search is just what the term implies—the Principal physically inspects the suspected target area to visually detect the presence of technical surveillance devices. A major prerequisite for conducting such a search is an understanding of how technical surveillance devices are employed and what they look like (see Chapter 3).

Surveillance devices can be disguised as almost anything and can be as small as a match head. The more sophisticated and easy to conceal, the more expensive the device will be. A surveillance team will assess the Principal's surveillance consciousness when determining what type of device to employ. If the Principal is a soft target and not assumed to be particularly suspicious of surveillance, it will normally opt to use a less sophisticated device. It will attack a hard target in a more secure and sophisticated manner. This is another example of why it is important that the Principal not alert a surveillance effort by exposing his surveillance detection activities.

Recall from Chapter 3 that a listening device will have a microphone, a power source, and a means of transmission. The power source will consist of alternating current (AC) or direct current (DC).

A device with a DC power source has a battery configuration attached. The more sophisticated or short-term the device, the smaller the battery. Since the surveillance team will require repeated access to the target area to resupply batteries, it may attach a parallel packet of batteries to extend the life of the device. This obviously makes the device larger and more readily detectable.

Using a device with an AC power source involves attaching it to the AC power circuit of the target area or running a separate wire to it through which electricity can be sent. Since it doesn't require batteries, an AC power source makes the device smaller and gives it virtually unlimited life. However, dependence on an AC power source gives the surveillance effort less flexibility in placing the device.

A listening device uses either radio frequency (RF) or wire for transmission. A RF device will have an antenna. Generally, the longer the antenna the better the range; miniature or built-in antennas significantly restrict the range of listening devices. Transmission frequency will also impact the length of the antenna. The longer the antenna, the bigger the listening device and, consequently, the more difficult to conceal. Additionally, principles of antenna propagation will limit how and where the listening device can be concealed. Wire transmission negates the need for an antenna, making the device relatively smaller. Although this may make the device easier to conceal, the wire attachment offers less flexibility in placement. (Review Chapter 3 for limitations involved in both RF- and wire-transmitted listening devices and how these can be exploited in technical detection activities.)

The physical inspection should be conducted so the surveillance effort cannot detect it and—since its purpose is to detect the presence of technical surveillance devices—under the assumption that the area is being monitored. Recall that often the surveillance effort will operate monitoring devices remotely, concentrating on those times that maximize the probability of successful interception. By using target pattern analysis, the Principal will assess the appropriate time to conduct the physical inspection based on when such monitoring of the target area is least likely to occur. This will generally be during normal sleeping hours.

As the area may be monitored by technical surveillance devices or other means, the Principal should disguise portions of the physical inspection with cover. This can consist of any measure that would project a plausible reason for activity that may be monitored during the search. Home-improvement projects or even housecleaning are examples. A stereo or television should be used to provide cover noise.

The Principal must conduct the physical inspection in a systematic manner to ensure that all possible locations are searched. When possible, he should use a construction diagram to identify features such as hollow walls, underfloors, or overhead accesses. If such a diagram is not available, he should develop a schematic that includes air handling ducts, conduit runs, and electrical wiring layout. The electrical wiring portion of the diagram must identify entry points. An entry point is any location where wiring or other types of conduit that could be used to power or transmit technical intercepts enter the target area. These consist primarily of electrical outlets, light switches, ceiling lights, and telephone line wall outlets.

The physical layout diagram should also detail the telephone system, including the makes and models of phones in the area, the locations of telephone entry points, and the locations of wire lines outside the area of interest. It should make note of computers and facsimile machines connected to telephone entry points, as well as all appliances connected to electrical entry points, such as televisions, radios, and lamps.

The inspection area should be divided into sections, normally by rooms. The Principal should inspect each section systematically, starting at a logical point—normally a doorway—and moving 360 degrees around the border back to the starting point. This search should extend from top to bottom. After completing the perimeter search, he should inspect the floor and all items in each of the areas. Finally, he should inspect the ceiling.

When inspecting the perimeter walls, ceiling, and floor, the Principal must uncover all entry points and inspect them to ensure that wiring configurations are appropriate and that no devices are connected at these points. Entry points provide quick and easy access to an electrical source for the emplacement of a technical surveillance device while also providing a degree of concealment. Since most listening devices and all video-monitoring devices emplaced in perimeter structures require a small hole, the Principal should inspect all areas for pinholes. Scanning an area with a flashlight in darkness is the easiest way to identify such holes. He should inspect any hole found to determine whether a microphone, camera, or tube lead is present. He should also inspect perimeter structures for variations in texture or paint that may be indicative of technical device emplacement. An ultraviolet light source is effective for this purpose. He should evaluate any variations he finds and inspect them for technical devices.

When the Principal identifies pinholes or structure variations, he should note the locations and inspect the perimeter from the exterior. This may be difficult if not impossible when the Principal does not have access to adjoining rooms, which is common in hotel rooms or offices that adjoin the target area from the sides, top, or bottom. He should inspect perimeters with denied external access thoroughly, because these are the most common locations for the emplacement of technical devices. This is because by gaining access to the exterior wall, the surveillance team can penetrate the exterior and emplace a device that is virtually undetectable. Operators can cut a drywall perimeter (characteristic of most hotels and office buildings), emplace a technical device, and cover it in a very short period. They can do this when an individual is in the room that is being attacked. When possible, the Principal should determine the identities of those controlling locations with external access to the possible target area. This may assist him in determining the feasibility of a technical attack from a given location.

Built-in wall units are effective locations for the emplacement of technical devices because of easy access and good concealment. Such structures should be inspected as if they were hard furniture (which will be addressed shortly) and for surface indicators as previously discussed.

The perimeter inspection should also include the removal of carpet to search for devices or wiring that are indicative of a technical attack. When it is impractical to remove the carpet, the Principal should probe the surface to feel for devices or wiring underneath. He should pull away wall-to-wall carpeting and inspect along the entire base perimeter of the wall. This is the most common location for the running of technical device wiring because it offers quick and effective concealment. He should remove all artwork and mirrors from the walls to ensure that they are not concealing alterations to the structure that are indicative of technical surveillance devices.

Because doors are normally hollow, providing easy access for the emplacement of listening devices, their interiors should be inspected thoroughly. The Principal can remove doorknob and keyhole assemblies to facilitate this. He should also inspect door casings and molding for indications of modification or removal. When appropriate, he should remove molding and inspect it.

Window locations require particular attention. Initially, all window coverings are commonly used as quick and effective locations for listening device emplacement. Drapes and curtains should be inspected thoroughly for sewn-in devices, as should blinds for any indication of built-in or emplaced devices. Window frame molding should be inspected for any indication of removal. Any molding that is used for decorative purposes or is easily removed should be inspected from behind. Molding should also be checked for pinholes and fine wires running along concealing crevasses.

The inspection of doors and windows should also include a search for indications of covert entry, such as unexplained chips in paint or indentations in wood. (Chapter 13, "Technical Antisurveillance," will address covert and forced entry in detail.)

After completing the interior perimeter inspection, the Principal should inspect the external perimeter for abnormalities that may be indicative of technical surveillance. Often this will be done in conjunction with the internal perimeter search of adjoining rooms. It should include the inspection of bordering insulation when applicable. All air and ventilation ducts leading into the area should be searched thoroughly for devices as well. These are particularly vulnerable because a listening device can be emplaced at virtually any point within the duct system. The Principal should conduct a thorough search of false ceiling paneling and overhead dead space if applicable. This will include inspecting paneling for hidden devices and paneling support wires for attached wiring that could serve as a technical device signal carrier.

Electrical and telephone wiring entering the area should be inspected thoroughly at every point to detect technical listening or transmitting devices. Ideally, this inspection will check the entire electrical and telephone system running through the residence or building, including intercom systems when applicable. Some knowledge of electrical and telephone wiring is required in order to identify abnormalities in the system. The inspection of telephone wiring should include any junction boxes outside the location and should extend to the public junction box servicing the entire area if possible. Again, when physical access to the entire electrical or telephone wiring system is not possible, there is a vulnerability to technical monitoring that cannot be discounted.

After completing this inspection, the Principal must inspect all items in the search area for the emplacement of technical devices. This should begin with a physical examination of all electrical appliances, and since technical devices are normally disguised as part of the appliance circuitry, some disassembly may be required. Next he should inspect all other items in the area systematically, moving 360 degrees from perimeter to center, as before.

An understanding of technical listening devices assists in this portion of the inspection. Such devices will normally be emplaced in locations that provide the least resistance to microphone effectiveness. Since hard structures significantly limit this effectiveness, it will generally be someplace that provides appropriate concealment while allowing effective interception, such as behind canvas pictures, inside stereo speakers, and inside stuffed or padded furniture. The Principal should inspect such locations thoroughly. He should check the fabric of stuffed furniture such as mattresses, chairs, sofas, and pillows to ensure that it has not been cut and resewn. This will include looking underneath dust covers, particularly characteristic of sofas, to ensure that they have not been removed and retacked. He should also probe all stuffed and padded furniture, checking for foreign objects that may be indicative of a technical listening device.

Hard furniture, such as metal and wooden desks and tables, should be physically inspected as well. Although it is difficult to place a device inside hard furniture without prior access, variations in surface paint or form may be indicative of technical device emplacement. Again, an ultraviolet light source will assist the Principal in detecting such surface variations. He should inspect all parts of the furniture, removing drawers and shelves and paying particular attention to detecting false concealment compartments in locations, such as desk drawers. He should also inspect furniture for metal items, such as extra braces that appear unusual.

Finally, the Principal should inspect all other items in the target area visually and physically. This will include a thorough search of books for hollowed compartments; all decorative items such as vases, baskets, and plants, which are common locations for listening devices; and items that might contain false bottoms or other fabricated concealment locations such as baskets, plants, and trash cans.

Telephones are of particular interest because of their vulnerability to technical manipulation. Without technical knowledge of the wiring of telephone units, physical inspection will only be effective in identifying emplaced listening devices. A wiring schematic for the phone unit will assist the Principal in identifying alterations to the wiring configurations. The search for such alterations should focus on those aspects of telephone microphone activation addressed in Chapter 3. This inspection will also include identifying any additional wires, capacitors, or resisters that may be emplaced to bypass microphone controls or enhance intercept quality.

TECHNICAL INSPECTION

Technical equipment can assist to varying degrees in the detection of technical surveillance devices. Such equipment ranges from reasonable to expensive, basic to sophisticated. The use of expensive equipment is limited by the available resources, while it is the expertise of the user that limits the use of sophisticated equipment. This section serves as an introduction to technical equipment and common applications.

The multimeter is the most basic type of technical detection equipment. Electricians commonly use this device to test electrical circuits. The multimeter is used primarily to measure voltage and resistance. Technical devices that draw on the power of a building or appliance will affect the standard level of voltage. For the purposes of surveillance detection, the multimeter measures electrical voltage to detect such a drain. Additionally, many technical devices use resistors or capacitors to regulate current for effective operation; the multimeter detects variations in resistance or voltage resulting from these peculiarities.

RF detection equipment is used to detect RF signals transmitted by technical surveillance devices. A primary limitation of this type of equipment is that a technical surveillance device must be active and transmitting before detection is possible. For this reason, the Principal should conduct RF detection activities at times he has assessed to be the most likely for a surveillance team to activate a device.

Countermeasures receivers are one category of RF detection equipment. The most basic of these is a commercially available frequency scanner; however, federal regulations restrict the frequencies these are able to detect. Therefore, since technical surveillance devices rarely operate on standard frequencies, frequency scanners offer only limited detection capability. More effective countermeasures receivers consist of wide-range RF receivers with the capability to demodulate signals across the spectrum of AM, FM, single-sideband, and continuous wave, to include subcarrier signals.

Another type of RF detection equipment is the spectrum analyzer. This device is set to search a specified frequency range for signals transmitting within that range. Output is displayed on a monitor that depicts the range under analysis and any signals detected. The spectrum analyzer is a relatively expensive piece of equipment, and using it to evaluate signals and determine whether they are generated by a technical surveillance device requires a degree of expertise. Many spectrum analyzers are capable of detecting the signals emitted from a microwave technical surveillance device. When compatible, countermeasures receivers can be coupled with a spectrum analyzer to provide a visual display of the specific signal under analysis.

The relative field strength meter is yet another type of RF detection equipment. It evaluates RF signal strength to determine the distance between the transmitting antenna and the detection activity. It can be used to track and isolate the source of the RF signal at issue. Many countermeasures receivers incorporate this field strength meter capability.

Once identified, RF signals can be further examined by an oscilloscope. The oscilloscope is used to observe wavelength forms and measure the voltage, time, frequency, and phase angle of signals.

Audio amplifiers form another category of technical detection equipment. These identify discussion or other types of audio that escape a designated area through air ducts, conduits, pipes, or even walls. This serves primarily to expose vulnerabilities that would allow a surveillance team to amplify and receive audio signals without having to gain access to the target area. Audio amplifiers can also be used to identify an active telephone microphone or to examine wires for transmitting listening devices.

Another piece of technical detection equipment is the Non-Linear Junction Detector. It consists of a transmitter that sends out UHF signals that return to a receiver when an object meeting specified harmonics criteria is detected. The Non-Linear Junction Detector is particularly effective in detecting semiconductor components, such as transistors, diodes, or integrated circuits, which are characteristic of technical listening devices. Since Non-Linear Junction Detectors react to device components rather than transmitted signals, they are capable of detecting inoperative or dead devices.

In many cases, detection equipment will identify anomalies within a structure that may be indicative of a technical surveillance device. Such indications may be inconclusive, however, due to the inherent limitations of detection equipment. The Principal can use portable X-ray equipment to examine such anomalies, rather than damaging the structure to uncover the source.

A technical inspection for the presence of technical surveillance devices will begin with RF detection. RF detection equipment employs a passive capability that gives operators monitoring a technical surveillance device no indication of the surveillance detection activity. The RF detection phase will include an online check of all telephones and connecting lines in the inspection area to identify audio signals leaving the area via telephone lines. Because the Principal will conduct this inspection while the telephone handset is in the cradle, surveillance operators monitoring a telephone bug or tap will not be alerted to the detection activity. Intercom systems can be manipulated in a manner similar to telephone bugging and should therefore be tested as potential audio carriers.

The remaining methods of technical surveillance detection may, to varying degrees, alert the surveillance effort to an ongoing technical inspection. The Principal must determine at this point whether the expected results warrant the risk.

As mentioned above, the Principal will use audio amplifier equipment to inspect pipes, ducts, and conduits that may carry conversation out of the target area. This requires that an audio source, such as a radio, be active in the suspected target area during the inspection. He will use Non-Linear Junction

Detectors to make a thorough inspection of the area, including walls, ceilings, floors, and all physical items within.

He will use the multimeter to inspect the electrical circuits and all appliances in the area. It is not necessary to detail that process here, as the multimeter user's manual should provide all of the information needed to conduct an inspection of the electrical wiring. Obviously, the manual will not specify the device's application to surveillance detection activity, but the same process electricians use to identify the source of an unexplained drain on a power line applies to detecting a technical surveillance device attached to a power line.

Wiring will be tested for voltage initially. If the Principal detects voltage, he will disconnect all power-consuming devices, such as appliances, from the line. He will then test the wire for current. If he detects it, he will physically inspect the run of the wire until he finds all legitimate power consumers or the technical surveillance device. He should test the current each time he disconnects a legitimate power consumer from the wire to ensure that an anomaly still exists. Electrical appliances are inspected in a similar manner, by disconnecting and testing the power cord to ensure that no foreign power loads exist within the appliance.

The multimeter is also used to inspect for the manipulation of a telephone unit. This requires an understanding of how a telephone is powered and how current flow is controlled through the unit. (Chapter 3 includes an overview of these principles.) The multimeter is used to determine whether current is activating any of the telephone microphones when the electrical circuit should be closed, which is indicative of technical manipulation.

One example of this multimeter application is to remove the transmitter microphone and measure its DC voltage potential while the hook switch is depressed. Any reading other than zero is indicative of technical manipulation. Other methods of bypassing circuit breaks to power a microphone may vary based on the wiring configurations of particular telephone models. Telephone repair manuals for specific makes will provide the wiring diagrams necessary to determine where and how to conduct voltage checks.

It is possible to detect concealed tape-recording devices with certain types of technical countermeasures equipment. A limitation of spectrum scanning equipment when used for this purpose is that the recorder must be operating in the record mode, when the erase head, or bias oscillator, emits a distinctive electromagnetic field that is susceptible to detection. Non-linear Junction Detectors can also be used to detect tape-recording devices.

The detection of surveillance monitoring devices is probably the easiest of any technical surveillance detection practice. Recall that monitoring devices consist primarily of beaconing systems, which are normally employed on a target vehicle. Although beacons can be well emplaced in the hardware of a vehicle, a surveillance team will rarely have the time and access to do so. Most beaconing systems are constructed to be mounted magnetically under the rear bumper of a vehicle to facilitate quick emplacement. This makes them easy for the security-minded Principal to detect.

Physically searching the vehicle is the primary method of detecting beaconing systems. The Principal should park in a concealed location, such as an enclosed garage, and search the vehicle's exterior systematically, concentrating initially on the bumpers and the wheel wells. Next he should inspect underneath the vehicle, including inside the tailpipe. Although an unlikely location for a beaconing device, the engine compartment should be inspected as well. The trunk should be inspected, and any liners that conceal hidden compartments removed. The Principal should also observe for reflective tape emplaced on the vehicle. When used by a surveillance team, reflective tape requires a line of sight; therefore, it will be visible on some portion of the vehicle's rear. Tape designed to reflect light is easily detectable. More sophisticated types of reflective tape that are only responsive to infrared light are more difficult to detect but still readily found by physical search.

Finally, the Principal should inspect the interior. He should observe for any indication that the roof insulation liner has been removed and replaced and probe the entire liner to detect a concealed beaconing device.

Chapter 3 addressed the employment of malicious software, particularly Trojan horses, for surveillance purposes. Measures to prevent the entry of malicious software into a computer will be discussed in Chapter 13, "Antitechnical Surveillance." In addition to the threat of malicious software, there is that of a surveillance team attempting to gain access to a target computer solely for information retrieval or data download. Recall that a computer in the stand-alone mode is much less vulnerable to penetration or malicious software than one that is networked into a computer system. This is because, in order to access a stand-alone computer, a surveillance operator must gain physical access to it, whereas he can conceivably access a computer on a network via any other computer on the system.

The Principal can take specific measures to detect unauthorized access or the presence of malicious software. The primary methods of detection involve the use of system security software. An inherent vulnerability of all computers is they are only as smart as the software that is installed. Therefore, a computer-literate surveillance operator who is smarter than the program can bypass or defeat any security control measure installed. Nevertheless, computer security software does enhance the ability to detect surveillance activities directed against a target computer.

The first surveillance detection measure to employ for computer security is an access monitoring system. Such a system identifies when computer access was attempted or accomplished and which files were opened. This is particularly important for a computer that is networked on a system. When protective measures, such as passwords, prevent access, the system will still record these unsuccessful attempts.

The most common computer security control measure used to support technical surveillance detection is antiviral software. This alerts the Principal to certain types of system access or manipulation that is indicative of typical malicious software. The many antiviral programs on the market vary widely in effectiveness. Those that only search a system for known viruses are of little use for surveillance detection purposes because a standard computer virus does not indicate a surveillance attack. Because a sophisticated surveillance effort will design a malicious software program that satisfies target-specific objectives, many antiviral software programs would not detect its presence. One way to counter this threat is through the use of system-sweep programs. These check files for changes in size, date, or content. This is an effective detection measure because it looks for indicators of malicious software in general rather than specific, previously identified viruses. High-quality antiviral programs will include a system-sweep application.

User awareness is the final way to detect indications of technical surveillance involving computers. Abnormal computer activity is but one indication of malicious software. All malicious software consumes computer memory, and some even replicates to destroy existing files. The Principal should observe for files, particularly systems operating files, that begin to consume additional memory. He should also maintain a log of access times and dates and compare it with the computer's internal log to detect unauthorized access.

CHAPTER 12

PHYSICAL ANTI-SURVEILLANCE

Antisurveillance consists of actions taken to elude or evade possible, suspected, or identified surveillance. Since surveillance is always possible, antisurveillance can be employed even when there is no specific indication that surveillance is present. The Principal will normally employ it to enhance security when he has reason to believe he is under surveillance and his activities must be protected. Espionage agents invariably follow this practice because of their extreme need to ensure that their activities go undetected. Although they may not have identified any indications of surveillance, the fact that it is always possible dictates that they employ antisurveillance before conducting any type of operational activity. This ensures that they will elude any possible surveillance effort before conducting activity that would provide evidence of illegal or operational activity.

Espionage agents are but one example of the many types of people who make antisurveillance a routine practice. Terrorists and sophisticated criminals use these same tactics. But antisurveillance is by no means restricted to the criminal element. U.S. Secret Service agents, bodyguards, and other protective services personnel make it a standard part of their executive security duties. In addition to making it a routine part of their jobs, they must be prepared to employ antisurveillance to the extreme of eluding a violent surveillance effort such as a terrorist attack.

As with all surveillance countermeasures, antisurveillance is based on an understanding of surveillance principles and tactics. The driving principle of most antisurveillance efforts is that a surveillance team will normally break contact with the Principal rather than accept a high risk of exposure. Most surveillance teams make operational security their highest priority, because if the Principal becomes aware of coverage, the surveillance effort is hindered severely if not rendered completely ineffective. Antisurveillance strives to capitalize on this by placing the surveillance team in a position that forces it to either terminate the surveillance or risk compromise.

An overt surveillance effort that is not concerned with compromise will require much more aggressive antisurveillance measures. This discussion is limited to antisurveillance principles and tactics as they apply to protecting personal privacy. Extreme antisurveillance measures, such as defensive driving to avoid a violent pursuit, are beyond the scope of this book. As is the case with surveillance detection, the number of possible antisurveillance maneuvers is unlimited. This chapter will focus on the principles that facilitate effective antisurveillance while addressing general tactical applications that should serve as a basis for understanding.

Many of the tactics used for surveillance detection can be applied effectively to antisurveillance. This relates to the principle that at some point the surveillance team must determine that the probability of compromise exceeds the benefit of continuing the surveillance operation. Surveillance detection tactics are executed for the purpose of placing a surveillance asset in a compromising position. A well-disciplined surveillance asset will normally make that split-second decision to break contact rather than risk exposure. This point illustrates that there is a vague distinction between many surveillance detection and antisurveillance maneuvers. The surveillance asset's reaction to a given maneuver—or decision not to react—may determine which surveillance countermeasures purpose the maneuver actually served.

Antisurveillance is the most difficult of the surveillance countermeasures to conduct discreetly. As with active surveillance detection, antisurveillance tactics range from discreet to overt. The more overt an antisurveillance tactic, the more effective it will be in eluding surveillance. At the same time, the more overt the tactic, the more aggressive and identifiable it will be to a surveillance team if present.

TARGET PATTERN ANALYSIS

The target pattern analysis process significantly enhances the effectiveness of antisurveillance. It identifies those activities the surveillance team will anticipate. As a surveillance operation progresses, the team identifies activities and patterns that are indicative of the Principal's intentions. When the Principal undertakes a unique activity or travel pattern, the surveillance team intensifies its coverage because it must be prepared to react to unanticipated actions. When the Principal's activity or travel pattern is consistent with past observations, the team tends to take a more conservative posture. This is due to the assumption that since the surveillance team is confident that it can anticipate the Principal's activity or travel destination it can loosen its coverage to decrease the probability of exposure. The team accepts this increased risk of losing command of the Principal because it is confident both of his destination and that if he is lost operators can simply relocate him there.

For example, if the Principal has established a pattern of taking the same route to work each day, the surveillance team will avoid the risk of undertaking aggressive maneuvers to maintain command of him because it assumes he will go to his workplace. If operators are forced to relinquish command due to traffic or other circumstances, they will simply travel to the assumed destination and reestablish the surveillance.

The Principal should base antisurveillance planning on target pattern analysis, which will identify the times and activities that may bring about a relaxation of the surveillance team's vigilance. The Principal will evaluate routes or circumstances that fit this profile and determine how antisurveillance applications can be incorporated most effectively. When he intends to conduct protected activity, he should begin his travels with a previously established pattern. At the appropriate time, he will conduct an antisurveillance maneuver that should catch the surveillance team off guard—enhancing the probability of success.

DISGUISE

Disguise can enhance antisurveillance because a surveillance team must recognize the Principal in order to follow him. A surveillance team relies primarily on features, form, dress, and mannerisms for recognition. It is difficult for operators to rely on features exclusively because this requires that they get too close to the Principal. Therefore, they will rely mostly on form, dress, and mannerisms. Recognition of form and mannerisms develops as the surveillance team has more opportunities to observe the Principal. Dress is a variable, but most people maintain a standard style of dress that makes them somewhat distinguishable. Many people also wear certain items such as coats, hats, and shoes with more regularity than others.

The Principal can manipulate the concepts of recognition that a surveillance team relies on to maintain observation. Surveillance operators establish a mental picture of the Principal based primarily on previous observations, and they come to rely on this to identify him. The Principal can deceive them by establishing an appearance that is not consistent with this frame of reference.

The Principal can employ any number of appearance alterations and disguise methods. Baggy or loose-fitting clothes can alter the form, and filling them out with materials to appear larger or bulkier will enhance this effect even further. Mannerisms can be altered by such methods as changing posture and pace of motion. Altering features is more complex and time-consuming. The simplest methods are to dye, cut, or restyle hair. This includes shaving any facial hair that might alter appearance significantly. Wigs offer another way to disguise hair. More complicated methods of altering features primarily involve applying facial makeup, which is available at any theatrical supply store.

Disguise is a very aggressive method of antisurveillance. If the surveillance team detects it, operators will be certain that the Principal has something to hide. The negative consequences of such a disclosure have been addressed thoroughly. Less overt methods of appearance alteration, such as wearing clothing that is inconsistent with the normal attire, do not present as significant a risk, but they are also less effective in eluding surveillance.

The Principal must ensure that the use of disguise is complete, because if the surveillance team detects it, antisurveillance is confirmed. This means that if the Principal alters one aspect of his appearance, he should make an effort to alter all aspects. It serves little purpose to alter facial appearance but wear clothes that the surveillance team would readily identify. Mannerisms are the most easily overlooked aspect of changing appearance. A surveillance team uses mannerisms such as bearing and pace of motion for recognition because these are unique to the Principal, remain consistent without a conscious effort to alter them, and can be observed from a distance. For this reason, it is essential that the Principal alter mannerisms to complement and make any other method of disguise effective.

STAKEOUT ANTISURVEILLANCE

Antisurveillance measures that can be taken against the possibility of a stakeout are limited because, as the Principal is virtually static at this point, there is little actual physical surveillance taking place other than containment. Inside a possible stakeout location, the Principal should conduct any protected activities in an area that precludes outside observation. Even inside a denied area a surveillance team may be able to observe the Principal's activities, primarily through windows. Because sophisticated observation equipment can penetrate curtained windows, and even the naked eye may be able to discern silhouettes, the Principal should conduct protected activities beyond a physical barrier.

Chapter 7 addressed the practice of alerting authorities to a suspected fixed or mobile observation post. Regardless of the result of the response to the call, if it is in fact an observation post, the surveillance team will consider the location or vehicle compromised and discontinue its use. This neutralization of the surveillance asset is an effective antisurveillance measure.

A primary consideration of the Principal's in employing antisurveillance tactics against a stakeout is that if he eludes a stakeout, he defeats surveillance. A stakeout is based on the assumption that the Principal will either depart or travel through a designated location. Based on this, the surveillance team will remain in the stakeout location until it observes the Principal. However, if he can elude the surveillance effort at the point of stakeout, he will be able to travel without the threat of surveillance. This is particularly so when the stakeout is based around a denied location that the surveillance team is certain the Principal is inside.

It is virtually impossible to depart a stakeout location by vehicle without detection. A vehicle can depart only by established roadways, and a surveillance team will certainly maintain observation of any possible routes of departure. One of the few possibilities for avoiding detection is when the stakeout location has a parking area that the surveillance team cannot observe, such as large business parking garages and secured compound facilities. A surveillance team depends significantly on the Principal's vehicle for identification of the Principal himself. It is normally difficult to observe each vehicle leaving a denied location and identify whether the Principal is the driver or a passenger. In fact, in many circumstances, although operators are unable to confirm that the Principal is driving his vehicle, they will pick up and follow it without hesitation, assuming he is inside as usual.

With this in mind, the Principal can elude surveillance by driving out of the denied location in a different vehicle than the one he used to enter. The use of disguise will make this virtually undefeatable. This tactic is used to bypass the stakeout and defeat that phase of the surveillance operation. Another option is to have someone drive him out of the denied area in a vehicle that is not known to the surveillance team. Again, the use of disguise will make this tactic virtually undefeatable, and if the Principal conceals himself by hiding in the trunk or ducking down in the seats, it will be absolutely effective.

A Principal can elude a stakeout by foot in many locations. Recall that a surveillance team will use target pattern analysis to determine its stakeout locations. When the Principal establishes a pattern of consistently departing a stakeout location in the same manner, the surveillance team will position assets accordingly. In some areas, such as residential neighborhoods, it is difficult if not impossible to maintain 360-degree observation coverage. For most residences, a surveillance team will only be concerned with the front of the location because most people depart from the front and will likely do so by vehicle. Based on this concept, the Principal will first analyze established patterns to predict how a surveillance team will position assets and then identify routes of departure that are unlikely or impossible for the surveillance team to observe. This allows him to depart the stakeout location undetected and conduct any activity without the risk of observation. With proper planning, he can do so and return without the surveillance team's ever realizing he was gone.

An example of the application of this tactic is when the Principal suspects that he is under surveillance and that his telephone is being monitored. Under such circumstances, he can depart the stakeout location covertly to make a telephone call that must be protected from eavesdropping and return undetected.

LOST COMMAND DRILL

The lost command drill is a surveillance technique that applies most specifically to antisurveillance. During the course of a follow, the surveillance team may lose command of the Principal for any number of reasons. When this occurs, unless the team is certain of the Principal's destination based on previous travel patterns or other sources, it will execute the lost command drill, a systematic sequence of maneuvers designed to regain command.

This drill consists of searching for the Principal along all possible routes originating from the first option encountered after lost command. When surveillance operators lose command of the Principal during the follow, they will continue aggressively in his last observed direction of travel in an attempt to reestablish command. When they reach a traffic option, they must conduct a lost command drill because, while the Principal may have continued straight at the option, there is also a possibility that he turned off. Committing surveillance assets to each possible route significantly degrades team integrity. Even when an operator reestablishes command of the Principal during this drill, he must continue the follow with a greater risk of exposure due to the degraded degree of team support. The fewer surveillance assets available at the outset to conduct the lost command drill, the proportionately lower the probability of success.

VEHICULAR ANTISURVEILLANCE

Recall that antisurveillance maneuvers will normally be based on target pattern analysis. The Principal will identify terrain that facilitates antisurveillance at locations identified during pattern analysis. Vehicular antisurveillance is restricted somewhat by the established avenues of travel and the maneuverability of vehicles. Antisurveillance tactics are based partially on an understanding of these limitations and how they also apply to surveillance vehicles.

The ability to accelerate quickly when necessary is a characteristic of vehicular travel that has a positive impact on antisurveillance. Fast and aggressive driving supports antisurveillance by making it difficult for a surveillance team to maintain integrity and command of the Principal. This also justifies making erratic maneuvers part of a standard driving pattern rather than using them only in antisurveillance efforts. Unanticipated maneuvers are the basis of antisurveillance because they force the surveillance team to either break contact or risk detection by reacting in a suspicious manner. A Principal who establishes a pattern of fast and aggressive driving has the flexibility to conduct more aggressive antisurveillance maneuvers without drawing as much suspicion.

The Principal vehicle's appearance has a significant impact on vehicular surveillance. Any unique feature that makes the vehicle easier to identify assists the surveillance effort. Conversely, a vehicle that blends with others on the road and has no distinguishing features such as dents, bumper stickers, distinctive license plates, or unique paint jobs is more difficult for the surveillance team to distinguish from similar models, which detracts from the effectiveness of surveillance and serves antisurveillance.

Understanding the lost command drill allows the Principal to exploit it, identifying locations that facilitate antisurveillance by enabling him to elude surveillance observation prior to a traffic option.

The most prominent of many such possible locations are those consisting of a blind approach to a traffic option. This is a bend or crest in the road that makes observation of the Principal difficult prior to the option. The Principal can use a blind approach most effectively in open terrain that forces the surveillance team to maintain a greater following distance for security. By accelerating when entering a bend in the road that obstructs the observation of following traffic, the Principal can turn off at an option before any possible following surveillance vehicle clears the bend. This will force the surveillance team to conduct a lost command drill at the option if it doesn't mistakenly disregard the possibility of a turn. This maneuver can be used in conjunction with any type of concealment the Principal can use to hide behind while the surveillance team unwittingly passes by. When appropriate concealment is not available, he should travel away quickly via an unlikely route.

In executing the lost command drill, the surveillance team may leave a vehicle at the point of lost contact in case the drill is unsuccessful. It can then attempt to reestablish command of the Principal should he pass back through the location. For this reason, any tactic that exploits the principles of the lost command drill should not include passing back through the point of lost command.

Traffic obstacles also support antisurveillance. It is difficult for a surveillance team to maintain command of the Principal when traveling through dense traffic. The Principal can apply this concept effectively by traveling through dense traffic, into a relatively open area, and then back into dense traffic. Breaking out of the dense traffic allows him to place distance between himself and the surveillance effort. By entering another area of dense traffic ahead of the surveillance effort, he can effectively lose surveillance. A more overt application of this tactic is to accelerate prior to entering the dense traffic. When breaking out of a dense traffic area, the Principal should use a route of departure that the surveillance team would not anticipate. This is based on the likelihood that the surveillance team will lose command of the Principal in the dense traffic and attempt to reestablish it after breaking free of the obstacle. To do so, the team must anticipate the Principal's likely route or possible routes of travel as addressed in the lost command drill. It may disregard less likely routes.

Traffic lights are another obstacle the Principal can use for antisurveillance. Particularly in dense urban traffic, they can facilitate antisurveillance by allowing the Principal to place distance between himself and the surveillance team before breaking out of the dense traffic area. By studying traffic light patterns, the Principal can travel in a manner that allows him to clear stop lights just before they turn red. A more overt tactic is to run a red light. Although this maneuver will certainly alert the suspicions of the surveillance effort, a surveillance vehicle will rarely risk detection by repeating this maneuver behind the Principal. Another option is to wait at the green light until it is about to turn red and then proceed. Again, this is an overt tactic, but the Principal can incorporate a somewhat plausible reason for it, such as reading a map or newspaper.

Trains can serve as obstacles to a surveillance effort as well. By crossing the tracks just before the train passes, the Principal can escape while following vehicles are obstructed from moving or observing beyond the train. International boundaries can serve the same purpose, because many surveillance teams will not cross international lines. Surveillance vehicles normally have unique equipment that will not pass the scrutiny of customs inspections. Even if the surveillance vehicle can be sanitized, the delay involved should give the Principal a sufficient lead on the surveillance team. Government law enforcement or investigative agencies must coordinate operations into another country; therefore, they would not continue the operation unless they knew the Principal's travel intentions in advance. Cross-country travel presents another obstacle to surveillance. Surveillance vehicles are selected based on their ability to blend with others on the road and will therefore be models designed for standard terrain. The Principal can use a four-wheel drive vehicle to travel across unimproved terrain and thereby evade surveillance.

Choke points and channelized terrain, as addressed in

Chapter 8, also facilitate antisurveillance. Choke points such as construction zones or toll booths are generally characterized by traffic obstacles that may allow the Principal to break away from the surveillance team, whose movement is obstructed. Channelized terrain normally forces the surveillance team to commit all of its assets to a single route behind the Principal.

Recall from Chapter 3 that a surveillance team will attempt to place surveillance vehicles on parallel routes in order to overcome any traffic obstacles encountered. Channelized terrain deprives the team of this flexibility in coverage. By drawing the surveillance team into channelized terrain, the Principal can use a traffic obstacle such as a stop light to obstruct the entire team while he escapes. Again, after the breakaway he should travel by a route that the surveillance team conducting a lost command drill would not anticipate.

During antisurveillance planning, the Principal must identify how he can exploit the characteristics of specific choke points. The concept of using dense traffic—which is characteristic of many choke points—to obstruct the surveillance team while quickly breaking out of traffic was addressed previously. A highway traffic jam presents another opportunity to apply this concept. Although it is illegal and perhaps a little dangerous, moving to the shoulder to bypass the traffic jam will allow the Principal to distance himself from the surveillance team. He should do this in a location that will allow him to reach a highway exit before the surveillance team has time to react. In very slow-moving, congested city traffic, the Principal can turn off the road at virtually any option and, unless they are directly behind him, prevent surveillance vehicles from following him until traffic allows them to reach the option.

Again, many of the tactics associated with vehicular surveillance detection are also effective antisurveillance maneuvers because the surveillance team may opt to break contact with the Principal rather than react in a detectable manner. Whenever a maneuver forces the surveillance team to break contact for security reasons, it is validated as an effective antisurveillance maneuver. Having achieved an understanding of antisurveillance principles and tactics, review the tactics addressed in Chapter 8, "Active Vehicular Surveillance Detection," from the perspective of how those maneuvers become effective antisurveillance measures if the surveillance team chooses to break contact rather than risk detection.

Anytime the Principal makes a turn, he forces the surveillance team to rotate command vehicle positions or risk detection by taking the turn directly behind him. The fewer surveillance vehicles involved in the follow, the less flexibility the team has to use such tactics. The Principal should identify logical routes of travel that incorporate successions of quick turns to exploit this vulnerability.

When he makes a 180-degree turn, the Principal forces the surveillance team to react immediately to avoid detection. Since most surveillance teams give discretion priority over maintaining command of the Principal, they will focus first on avoiding detection. This in itself makes a 180-degree turn an effective anti-surveillance tactic.

Another possible tactic is a 180-degree turn consisting of exiting a highway and taking the overpass to reenter in the other direction. An overt variation of this is to take a highway exit where traveling to the overpass is an option. The Principal will stop at the option, allowing any following surveillance vehicles to close in. Then, rather than turning in the direction of the overpass, which is normally left, the Principal will turn and travel away from it. After traveling a short distance (but out of sight of the overpass), he will execute a 180-degree turn and return to the highway. This maneuver will enable him to reach and reenter the highway traveling in any direction, unobserved by the surveillance team, which is reacting to the 180-degree turn. This forces the team to split in two directions to reestablish contact with the Principal, who by that time should have established a substantial lead. The Principal should take the next possible exit and travel again along an unlikely route. The less time the surveillance team has to catch him before he exits, the better. Again, fast driving enhances the effectiveness of the maneuver. This tactic is applicable to many city street options as well.

Service roads that allow authorized vehicles to turn around on a highway by crossing the median can serve as overt yet very effective antisurveillance routes. The Principal should identify the locations of service roads to determine which are appropriate for antisurveillance. The most effective locations will allow the Principal to execute a 180-degree turn on the highway and travel only a short distance before he has an opportunity to turn off the highway and escape along an unlikely route.

An even more overt variation of this tactic is for the Principal to execute a 180-degree turn and then pull over in the breakdown lane of the highway facing in the other direction. By stopping within observation range of the service road, he forces any following surveillance vehicle to continue past it rather than repeat this overt maneuver within his observation range. This ensures that a surveillance vehicle cannot use the service road to execute a 180-degree turn after the Principal is out of observation range, as is possible with the first method. Yet another variation of this is for the Principal to stop in the breakdown lane of the highway just prior to the service road. After waiting a short time to allow any following surveillance vehicles to pass by, he reenters the highway and executes the 180-degree turn on the service road.

Another overt highway antisurveillance method is for the Principal to exit the highway on a ramp and immediately stop in the breakdown lane of that ramp. After waiting a short time to allow any following surveillance vehicles to exit the highway and pass by, he will carefully back up in the breakdown lane to reenter the highway. A variation of this is to stop in the breakdown lane immediately after passing an exit and, after allowing any following surveillance vehicles to pass by, back up and take the highway exit.

The Principal should make use of his knowledge of how a surveillance team reacts to a stop during the mobile follow. Recall that the surveillance team will attempt to position a vehicle in a static position to observe the Principal when stopped. The remaining surveillance vehicles will maneuver to establish box positions along his possible routes of departure. The surveillance team will position assets along these routes, prioritizing them according to which the Principal is most likely to take. When there are not enough surveillance vehicles to cover all of the possibilities, less likely routes will go unboxed, creating holes through which the Principal can escape. For this reason, when departing the location of a stop, the Principal should travel away along an unlikely route. In many cases, this may involve making an immediate 180-degree turn in order to travel away in the direction from which he approached. This maneuver is particularly effective when followed by a quick turn, or succession of turns, off the established route of travel.

In selecting the appropriate stopping location for antisurveillance purposes, the Principal should identify one that offers no inconspicuous locations for the surveillance team to position a vehicle for observation. If the surveillance team has no discreet options for a trigger position, it will normally forego positioning a vehicle that would be vulnerable to detection. At this point the team will focus on positioning vehicles along possible routes of departure. This puts the surveillance team at a significant disadvantage because operators will be unable to observe the Principal until they pick him up along a given route of travel—if there is a surveillance vehicle covering that route. Again, the surveillance team may be forced to leave less likely routes of departure unboxed due to limited resources. In this situation, by taking an unlikely or unanticipated route, the Principal can depart the stop location without the surveillance team's knowledge.

A surveillance team should react to a stop by the Principal in a secure and systematic manner. At this point, the team must maneuver to box positions by routes that are undetectable by the Principal. This is rarely an instantaneous process. By stopping just long enough to force the surveillance team to initiate the boxing process and disperse, the Principal may be able to maneuver away by a route that is not yet covered.

Many of the previously addressed tactics involving stops on the highway are applicable to city antisurveillance as well. Stopping on channelized terrain and then executing a U-turn after following vehicles have passed is one example. The Principal can also stop immediately after passing an intersection and back up or turn around to take one of the other routes off the intersection after vehicles have passed. Again, this maneuver is most effective in channelized terrain.

One final vehicular antisurveillance tactic exploits a surveillance team's anticipation that the Principal will stop. Again, based on insight gained in target pattern analysis, the surveillance team will attempt to minimize exposure by relaxing coverage when the Principal's destination is obvious. Understanding this, the Principal can exploit it for antisurveillance purposes. Since a surveillance team is particularly vulnerable when the Principal stops and departs his vehicle with an enhanced field of vision, it will identify when this is likely to occur and alter coverage accordingly to enhance security. As mentioned earlier, the residence and workplace are the most common such locations, but the Principal's travel patterns dictate the number of possibilities.

As it identifies appropriate locations, the surveillance team will normally establish a point prior to the assumed destination at which to terminate coverage. This enables operators to begin establishing a surveillance box without committing a surveillance vehicle past the destination and thus unnecessarily exposing a surveillance asset. By assessing locations at which the team is likely to terminate coverage, the Principal can facilitate antisurveillance by traveling to the location and then continuing past it.

FOOT ANTISURVEILLANCE

Antisurveillance by foot is much more difficult than by vehicle in open terrain, mainly because of the limitations of speed and maneuverability. By foot, the slower speed of travel makes it easier for surveillance operators to react to the Principal's movements in a natural manner. Additionally, the effectiveness of virtually all vehicular antisurveillance maneuvers can be attributed to the restricted maneuverability—due primarily to established roads—surveillance vehicles face after the Principal executes a maneuver. Since foot surveillance operators encounter few of the obstacles and restrictions that vehicles do, they are better able to overcome similar antisurveillance maneuvers by the Principal on foot. This increased maneuverability can, however, facilitate the Principal's antisurveillance efforts when exploited effectively.

The previous section emphasized the principle that most surveillance detection maneuvers may also be effective antisurveillance maneuvers, depending on the reaction of the surveillance team. This is much less applicable to foot antisurveillance because the limitations to observation that restrict foot surveillance detection maneuvers also restrict their effectiveness when applied toward antisurveillance. Recall that the three primary things to be exploited in foot surveillance detection are turns, stops, and public locations. The tactics involved here are integral to antisurveillance as well, but their applications differ considerably.

By foot the Principal can exploit blind turns (as defined in Chapter 9), which are characteristic of virtually any downtown city block, to facilitate antisurveillance. He should identify such locations in advance. By taking a blind turn and then taking another immediate turn while obstructed from the view of any possible surveillance operators, the Principal can elude surveillance. Public locations, such as stores, are common turning locations that are readily available after blind turns. Public locations that have an exit other than the door through which the Principal entered are particularly conducive to executing this tactic effectively. This enables the Principal to depart the location and escape by a route that is unobservable by surveillance operators traveling along the previously established route.

The exploitation of pedestrian traffic is the most discreet method of foot antisurveillance. A foot surveillance operator's observation is restricted by line of sight. Pedestrian traffic creates a natural obstacle to both the vision and movement of surveillance operators. By moving from a relatively open area that forces surveillance operators to distance themselves and into a congested pedestrian location, the Principal can readily elude observation.

In many public locations there is a high concentration of people, allowing the Principal to blend into the crowd and disappear. Often public locations are also conducive to antisurveillance because they have multiple exits by which the Principal can escape after entering. When the Principal enters a public location, there will normally be a short delay before a surveillance operator enters, due to the coordination involved. This period of lost command allows the Principal time to maneuver to elude surveillance. Building on this idea, when the Principal enters a public location, it will take some time for the surveillance team to identify and cover all exits to the location from the outside. Also, the number of exits it can cover is limited by the number of operators. The Principal should exploit these vulnerabilities by departing the location quickly by an unlikely or difficult-to-find exit.

The previously addressed concepts of using channelized terrain and choke points also apply to foot antisurveillance. Although these features are not limited to public establishments, such locations do provide a proportionately higher number of natural choke points and channelizing options. These characteristics are readily identified in examining public locations for antisurveillance applications during the planning phase.

Elevators, available in many public locations, are one type of channelized terrain that places unique restrictions on a surveillance team. To follow the Principal on an elevator, a surveillance operator must get dangerously close. With a suspected surveillance operator on the elevator, the Principal can employ more overt tactics to elude surveillance. He should not select a level until all occupants have chosen their destinations. He should observe which levels specific individuals select so he can subsequently identify anyone who does not disembark at the level selected—making this an effective surveillance detection tactic as well. After all others on the elevator have selected their destinations, the Principal will select any level that was not chosen. If this option does not exist, he should select the top level. By departing at a level that no one else selected, the Principal will elude any potential surveillance operator—unless that operator compromises security and disembarks with the Principal, thus serving surveillance detection purposes. When the Principal is forced to select the top level because no other option exists, an overt method of antisurveillance is to remain on the elevator after it has reached the top. Any surveillance operator who remains with the Principal at this point has no regard for security and should be considered a threat. At the first indication that the other individual intends to remain on the elevator as well, the Principal should exit immediately and aggressively elude him because of the threat of attack.

If the surveillance team does not place a surveillance operator on the elevator, it will lose command of the Principal and have a degree of uncertainty regarding his intentions. Even when operators are able to observe the level indicator light, they cannot be certain whether the Principal disembarks when the elevator stops or if the stop is for other individuals to enter or exit. At this point the Principal can take the elevator to an appropriate level and then elude surveillance by exiting via a different route. The surveillance team will establish a trigger on the ground floor elevator, anticipating the Principal's eventual return.

Subway stations provide a high concentration of people, choke points, and channelized terrain. These locations give the Principal an opportunity to blend with the populace while moving to high-speed avenues of escape in the subway trains. Subway stations impose unique restrictions on a surveillance team because it is virtually impossible to maintain team integrity in such an environment. Although an overt antisurveillance tactic in design, multiple changes between subway trains will further degrade the team's integrity and eventually make continued surveillance impossible without detection.

When traveling by any mode of public transportation, the overt methods of antisurveillance are limitless. One primary consideration in this regard is that, when the surveillance team loses the Principal when he is traveling by public transportation, it will normally return to the location of lost command in anticipation that he will eventually return via the same route. In order to avoid this standard lost command stakeout tactic, the Principal should return via an alternate route, unless it is appropriate for him to pick up surveillance again to decrease the team's suspicion of antisurveillance tactics. He can also commission a taxi driver to conduct antisurveillance maneuvers, as detailed in Chapter 8.

Any location that incorporates specific types of security measures is effective for antisurveillance. This is based primarily on the fact that a surveillance team is not only concerned with detection by the Principal but also by third parties. Security personnel or systems provide the third party for antisurveillance purposes. Even a surveillance team that is operating under official authorization must be sensitive to compromise by well-intentioned security personnel. Security personnel are trained and employed to identify suspicious activity, rendering any surveillance team vulnerable to detection. Additionally, security systems such as X-ray machines and metal detectors will obstruct or delay the entry of surveillance operators with communications equipment or firearms. Through prior planning, the Principal can exploit such locations for antisurveillance purposes.

COMBINED FOOT AND VEHICULAR ANTISURVEILLANCE

Combined foot and vehicular surveillance requires that the surveillance team switch from a vehicular surveillance to a foot surveillance, or vice versa. During these periods of transition, a surveillance team must move foot operators out of or into a vehicle, normally after the Principal has already begun or completed this change. The process is further complicated by the fact that the surveillance team must accomplish it in a secure manner that is unobservable by the Principal.

If the surveillance team is unable to anticipate the Principal's actions and effect a smooth and secure transition, it will have difficulty maintaining command. The Principal will exploit these vulnerabilities for antisurveillance purposes. By planning such transitions, the Principal will be able to select locations that enable him to make them quickly while limiting the surveillance team's ability to do so, such as one that allows him to park his vehicle and travel quickly into a densely trafficked area. The possibilities are limitless but might also include traveling quickly into a public location with multiple exits or onto a mode of public transportation such as a subway train.

The surveillance team may establish a box around the Principal vehicle, particularly when he is on foot and unseen. This offers the team a measure of control, since it assumes the Principal will eventually return to his vehicle. Regardless of the boxing activity, the surveillance team's focus will still be on following or finding the Principal while on foot. Surveillance vehicles will support the foot operators, as necessary, both when they have command of the Principal and when they are searching for an unseen Principal.

This makes the team vulnerable to a quick transition back to a vehicular surveillance. The Principal should plan his travels in a manner that enables him to return to his vehicle while unobserved by the surveillance team or with little indication of his intentions to travel away by vehicle. Either of these circumstances will require that the surveillance team switch to the vehicular follow hastily. This may result in the Principal's driving away along a route that is not yet boxed. It may also force the surveillance team to transition to the vehicular follow before it has the opportunity to pick up its foot operators.

As a result, surveillance vehicle drivers will be conducting the follow without navigators, which will require them to perform the functions of the navigator, including reading a map and transmitting information, while driving. Anytime a surveillance vehicle is forced to operate without a navigator, team effectiveness is degraded and maintaining command of the Principal becomes much more difficult. This in effect serves the purposes of antisurveillance.

DUSK/DARKNESS ANTISURVEILLANCE

Dusk and darkness provide natural concealment that the Principal can use for antisurveillance purposes by both foot and vehicle. Darkness is a significant asset in eluding surveillance by foot. By traveling through poorly lit areas, he can readily escape by any number of options. A primary consideration, however, is that unless it is a normal aspect of the Principal's travel patterns, such an activity will certainly raise the suspicion of a surveillance team if present. A surveillance team following the Principal under these circumstances will probably assume that he intends to engage in protected activity due to the peculiarity of the situation and may intensify coverage in anticipation of this. Additionally, a surveillance team may employ night vision devices to degrade the concealment advantages darkness provides.

Darkness gives the Principal traveling by vehicle a significant advantage over a possible surveillance team. Recall from Chapter 8, which addressed many concepts applicable to physical vehicular antisurveillance at night, that a primary consideration is to drive a vehicle that does not have a unique or readily distinguishable rear light signature. At night, a surveillance team must rely on this feature for recognition, so by projecting a signature that blends in with those of other vehicles on the road, the Principal is more capable of effective antisurveillance. In dense traffic, it is difficult for a surveillance team to maintain command of the Principal if he does not have a unique rear light profile. The Principal can maneuver through dense traffic to make it impossible for the team to distinguish his rear light signature from that of other vehicles on the road. The tactics associated with accelerating when entering and breaking out of dense traffic are equally effective at night.

In open or desolate areas the Principal should exploit the restrictions imposed on a surveillance team. The open terrain, which makes following surveillance vehicles detectable from a greater distance by the projection of their headlights, forces them to increase their following distance. This increases the Principal's antisurveillance options. The previously addressed tactic of accelerating after entering a blind bend or hill in the road becomes even more effective with the increased following distance night surveillance dictates. An overt tactic the Principal can employ in this situation is to kill the vehicle lights after eluding the line-of-sight observation of all following vehicles. Through previous planning, the Principal will have identified an appropriate location to turn into that will be undetectable to following vehicles. To negate the effectiveness of a surveillance box along the previously established route, the Principal should depart the area by another route.

CHAPTER 13

ANTI-TECHNICAL SURVEILLANCE

Surveillance countermeasures employed to prevent vulnerabilities to or neutralize the effectiveness of technical surveillance capabilities are called antitechnical surveillance. Except in the rare circumstance of actually discovering a technical surveillance device, antitechnical surveillance involves measures taken to prevent a possible current or future technical surveillance attack. This is normally a standard security practice undertaken with no information to indicate that a specific technical threat exists. The cautious Principal always assumes that surveillance activity is possible and may likely go undetected. Given this assumption, he will practice antitechnical surveillance as a precautionary measure to enhance the integrity of personal privacy and security.

When a technical surveillance device is discovered during the technical surveillance detection inspection (Chapter 11), the Principal has the choice of leaving the device in place or neutralizing it. If he decides to neutralize it, he will take an active antitechnical surveillance measure, which will normally consist of removing the device and rendering it inoperative.

As with all surveillance countermeasures, antitechnical surveillance is based on an understanding of opposition technical surveillance capabilities, as addressed in Chapter 3. Even the most thorough of technical surveillance detection inspections cannot ensure security from a technical surveillance attack. The more sophisticated the technical surveillance capability, the more difficult it will be to detect. Many devices are designed specifically to bypass the scrutiny of a technical surveillance detection inspection. Based on this threat, the Principal will take measures to prevent the possibility of a technical attack and to neutralize a possible current attack.

Again, target pattern analysis will focus the antitechnical surveillance activities. The Principal will assess where he is vulnerable to a technical attack and in which locations a surveillance team would likely employ a technical surveillance capability to maximize the possibility of information gain—normally, the residence and workplace. In making this assessment, the Principal will further isolate specific areas or rooms within the location that are more probable targets of a technical attack because of their physical characteristics or the activities conducted therein. Vulnerability to technical surveillance generally does not extend beyond a target location because of the measure of security provided. To observe or record the Principal's activities by technical means, the surveillance team must identify a location where protected activity will most likely be conducted. Because of this and the limitations involved in the emplacement of a technical surveillance capability, the team must identify a fixed location from which the activity to be monitored can be collected. This restricts the surveillance team to the use of a target area.

There will be some vulnerabilities outside of a specific location, but normally only a few unless unique circumstances exist. One example of such a vulnerability is the possibility of a monitoring capability on a vehicle. Chapter 11 addressed the inspection of a vehicle to detect such a device. To emplace a beaconing device, the surveillance team would need to gain access to the vehicle. Therefore, the primary antisurveillance measure is to protect the vehicle from access. The Principal should park it in a secure, enclosed location, such as a garage, when it is not in use. He can also install a perimeter sensor alarm system to deter access to the vehicle when it is not in an enclosed location. Another such measure is to avoid leaving the Principal vehicle overnight when taken for mechanical servicing, as this would provide a surveillance team with the time and access necessary to emplace a beaconing device that would be impossible to detect by physical inspection. The surveillance team could either commission the cooperation of the service station owner or gain access by covert or forced entry. Another physical monitoring threat consists of chemical compounds a surveillance team can place on a vehicle to monitor its movements with an infrared sensor. A good car wash will neutralize this threat.

Another vulnerability that will extend beyond the target area and the Principal's control involves telephone tapping. The Principal will rarely have the opportunity to inspect neighborhood junction boxes or the telephone lines leaving the immediate workplace and running out to the office building junction. Due to the increased interest in competitive and economic intelligence, many businesses take measures to protect the security of their operations. Many of these measures, such as telephone security practices, may reduce the Principal's overall vulnerability. Even when the telephone lines outside the target area can be inspected, they can rarely be protected. An inspection will only detect an ongoing telephone tap or indications of a previous one; this does not preclude subsequent telephone tap emplacement.

Regardless of the measures taken, any conversation that takes place on a standard telephone is vulnerable to interception. For this reason, a basic antitechnical surveillance measure is to avoid discussing any protected information over a telephone. Using a push-to-operate telephone handset is another. Any standard telephone handset contains a receiver and transmitter microphone, one of which would be manipulated in a telephone bugging attack. The push-to-operate handset defeats a technical bypass effort (see Chapter 3) by electrically disconnecting the microphone unless the control button is depressed. There are handsets available that disconnect one or both of the microphones. Any efforts to manipulate the handset to enable a microphone to transmit will be detectable during a telephone conversation. Push-to-talk handsets neutralize a manipulated phone's function as a listening device when it is not in use, but they do not protect telephone conversations from tapping.

The only way to ensure the security of a telephone conversation is to use a telephone unit with an encryption capability. This is a telephone that transmits conversation in the form of an encrypted electrical energy code. The primary limitation of using a secure telephone is that both parties to the conversation must have compatible units in order to decrypt and understand the encoded transmissions. A telephone encryption device does not completely elude a surveillance effort if the line is being tapped. The monitoring surveillance asset will not be able to understand what is being said, but due to the unique tone passing through the lines, it will be aware of the fact that an encrypted conversation is taking place. The surveillance team can identify the specific telephone used by individuals with whom the principle has protected conversations by employing a line decoder system or other technical analysis techniques.

Foreign intelligence services collect much of the business-related information they need for economic espionage by intercepting facsimile transmissions. Fax transmissions have the same vulnerabilities as telephone conversations, but the unique characteristics of their microwave signal enable them to be more readily identified and isolated for intercept. Fax machines are available with encryption features, but again the receiving machine must have a compatible decryption capability.

The physical security of the possible target location is a primary consideration in antitechnical surveillance. In some circumstances, such as when at the workplace, the Principal will have little control over this. The nature of many businesses dictates that they employ physical security measures that are more than adequate. Understand, however, that if the Principal is the target of a government investigative or law enforcement agency, the opposition may gain entry to the workplace to launch a technical surveillance attack with the cooperation of the employer. Additionally, employers are increasing the use of technical surveillance methods in the workplace to monitor employee performance.

In determining the feasibility of conducting a technical attack on a target location, the surveillance team will examine the risk involved with entering to emplace a technical surveillance device. Prior to any attempt at entry, the surveillance effort will conduct a thorough reconnaissance of the target location.

The physical surveillance of the Principal will support this effort by informing the reconnaissance team of when he is away from the residence. This type of support will extend through the reconnaissance and continue when the actual entry takes place.

Effective physical security measures serve primarily to prevent or detect an entry attempt in progress, but also to deter such an operation. Any surveillance effort that is concerned with the security of its operation will undertake an entry attempt for a technical attack only when the probability of detection is minimal. Physical security measures that are apparent to the surveillance reconnaissance team may be enough to deter any further consideration of a technical attack.

The effectiveness of physical security measures will vary based on the surveillance team's degree of sophistication in covert entry techniques. Virtually any security system can be bypassed given the necessary time and expertise. The presence of a dog is one variable to the security of a location that will often serve as the primary deterrent to breaking and entering. National statistics on crime disclose that burglars will automatically forego any attempt at breaking and entering at a location with a dog. This applies even if the dog's bark is worse than its bite, because there are few alarm systems more reliable than a barking dog.

The methods of entry a surveillance team uses to access a target area are similar to those used by many criminals. The primary difference is that a surveillance team will rely almost exclusively on covert methods to ensure that the Principal does not know the location has been compromised. A discussion of the types of security systems and measures as they apply to the methods of breaking and entering are beyond the scope of this chapter. Appropriate physical security practices should be determined through the research of opposition breaking and entering techniques and the advice of physical security consultants.

One final consideration here is that a surveillance team may conduct an overt forced entry that appears to be a standard burglary. This may occur when the surveillance effort determines that a covert entry is not possible due to the time required or the security measures in place. The surveillance effort will assume that stealing objects from the target location to disguise the attack as a burglary will cause the Principal to discount the possibility of a technical attack.

Many antisurveillance measures will be incorporated into the technical surveillance detection inspection as it is conducted. A basic countermeasure is to cover detected pinholes with plaster. Any unnecessary telephone or electrical wires discovered during the inspection should be removed as well, as should mirrors and other large metal reflective surfaces that can be exploited through the use of laser systems. Telephone junction boxes should be locked.

A number of countermeasures can be incorporated into a potential target area for antisurveillance. An extreme example is the use of structural fortifications to protect against audio leakage. Windowless rooms are much less vulnerable to the threat of directional microphones, laser beam systems, and enhanced optical devices. When windows are present they should be covered by shutters or heavy lined drapes. This also decreases the quality of audio intercept from window glass vibrations.

Music masking can be used to conceal audio leakage that is detected by an audio amplifier or other means. Audio can escape a target area via pipes, conduits, air ducts, or simply through walls. Music masking distorts audio leakage by transmitting music through a network of speakers placed close to and facing the source of leakage. Radio or commercially programmed music should not be used for masking. The reason for this is that by identifying the music used for masking, such as a local radio station, the surveillance team can record the same radio station transmissions and use them to filter the masking music out of audio intercepts. Alternatives to the use of commercially programmed music that can be similarly acquired and used for filtering include compiling a tape of various songs that would be difficult to duplicate. ("Elevator" or "dentist's office" music is a good example of such products.) Another option is the use of classical music, which, although readily identifiable by composition, is difficult to distinguish by artist or recording product.

The acoustics of the target area affect the quality of a technical listening device. All items in a target area absorb sound to varying degrees. Soft items, such as stuffed or padded furniture, absorb sound much better than hard ones, such as wooden or metal furniture, which reflect rather than absorb much of the sound waves when contacted. The absorption of sound in the target area, however, does not degrade the effectiveness of a listening device because the necessary audio is received and transmitted before being absorbed. In fact, the absorption of audio improves the quality of intercept.

Sound waves that bounce off hard surfaces rather than being absorbed produce secondary noise that distorts the quality of a technical listening device intercept. A common example of this phenomenon is the echo that occurs when talking in an empty room. For this reason, an area used for protected conversations should have as few items in it as possible, and only hard items if any. Additionally, the fewer items inside a potential target area, the fewer the options for the emplacement of a technical surveillance device.

A surveillance team may attempt to introduce a technical surveillance device into a target area by means that do not require physical access. An example is sending gifts or promotional products to the Principal that are accepted into the target area. The Principal should exercise caution when offered such items and investigate their source. Another example of this technique is for the surveillance team to discover that the Principal has an item on layaway at a department store. By gaining access to the item by covert entry or another means, the surveillance team can emplace a technical surveillance in it that may bypass the Principal's scrutiny. The methods are virtually unlimited.

Anyone with access to a potential target area, such as service and custodial personnel, should be regarded with caution. The Principal should investigate the bona fides of any such personnel to ensure that they are credible. Understand, however, that before attempting to emplace a technical device by this method, a sophisticated surveillance team may establish a cover to protect the security of the operation. This could include establishing a bogus agency to lend an air of legitimacy to individuals who claim to be employees. In any case, the Principal himself should undertake any recommended repairs or modifications within a potential target area when possible. For example, when a telephone repairman determines that a phone needs to be replaced and offers to do so, the Principal should deny this offer and purchase a phone himself. When the recommended service is beyond the Principal's capability, he should defer its implementation pending a second professional opinion.

A surveillance team may recruit housekeepers or office employees to support the emplacement of a technical surveillance device in a target area. The team may use unfaithful employees to either emplace a device or grant operators access to the target area. It is not uncommon for less scrupulous surveillance elements to develop exploitable information with which to blackmail an employee into supporting the technical surveillance effort.

A surveillance team assesses potential target locations to determine whether the benefit expected from the emplacement of a technical monitoring device is greater than the risk involved. This assessment is based on the probability that the Principal will conduct protected conversations or activities at a given location. An antitechnical surveillance measure that can be used to circumvent the threat of technical listening is to conduct protected conversations in locations that a surveillance team would not consider for a technical attack, based on target pattern analysis. The Principal can use this method for personal or telephone conversations, but he must ensure that the location he selects is not vulnerable to directional microphone monitoring or optical device observation.

There are a number of antitechnical surveillance measures the Principal can use to protect computers from surveillance. Antitechnical surveillance measures associated with computer security consist primarily of access control methods designed to deny unauthorized individuals access to the information stored in the computer's files. The first level of access control is the physical security of the computer's location. This is a significant aspect of stand-alone computer security, but recall that there are many less intrusive methods of accessing a computer in a networked configuration.

Virtually all access control measures, other than physical security, are programmed into the computer. The most basic of these is the use of a password—a word or code that must be typed into the computer before access to the system is granted. This should be the only access control measure necessary for most stand-alone computers, provided that the Principal commits the password to memory and does not write it down or divulge it to anyone else. A computer technician can defeat a password through trial and error or by attaching a computer with a program that performs the same function, only more quickly. Either method requires a degree of time and access to a computer in a denied area—which is uncommon. An additional control measure to counter these methods of unauthorized access is a program that instructs the computer to shut down for a designated period of time after three unsuccessful password attempts.

A target computer in a networked configuration is significantly more vulnerable to unauthorized access because, conceivably, it can be accessed via any other computer on the system. Additionally, a surveillance team can introduce a computer to the network at any point along the transmission lines. Since computers are normally networked over standard telephone lines or by similar means, a surveillance team can access a target computer without having to bypass physical security and risk physical presence in a denied area. Penetrating a network for this purpose follows the same principles as telephone tapping.

The purpose of networked computer systems is to facilitate the open exchange of information. This very factor is incompatible with the principles of access control. On networked systems, access controls can be implemented only when all system users share the same concern for security and can be trusted. The most effective measure of system security is encrypted interface and data transfer. This is an expensive and complicated proposition which requires that all computers on the system have a compatible encryption capability.

Security measures on a networked system, if present, are normally limited to the use of passwords. Regardless of the application, a target computer on a networked system is still significantly vulnerable to surveillance. As previously explained, a computer technician or program can be employed to bypass a password system given time and access, which is as simple as gaining access to the computer network at any point. Again, an automatic shutdown access control measure can counter this specific application, but it is not foolproof. With access to the network transmission lines, a surveillance team can also evaluate recorded computer access transmissions to determine how to gain access. This in effect provides the surveillance team with the password and open access to the system.

One countermeasure that will decrease the vulnerabilities inherent in a password network is tiered access control, which denies access to certain protected files. It allows password users to gain access to only those files the Principal wants open to the network and denies access to the others. The vicious cycle continues, however, because for virtually any access control measure incorporated into a network there is a penetration measure to defeat it. One way to penetrate the tiered access control system is to introduce a Trojan horse program with a trapdoor through the network into the open access files. The malicious code can be programmed to attach to the restricted files immediately when the Principal accesses them. At this point the trapdoor will grant the surveillance team access to the restricted files at any time.

The previous example is not the only way to introduce malicious software into a target computer. A common method is to identify a personal or professional interest of the Principal's and develop a program with a malicious trapdoor code compatible with that interest. The software will be provided to the Principal as a promotional offer or by other appropriate means. The software need only be introduced into the target computer once, and the malicious code will attach to the system's permanent memory. Many sophisticated malicious software programs are developed to attach to another file when the ones they are on are about to be deleted. To counter this threat, the Principal should use only prepackaged software developed by established companies and acquired under controlled circumstances. He should avoid pirated software and shareware.

All computers radiate electromagnetic pulses when in use. These emissions are referred to as compromising emanations. Although they can be captured and intercepted by technical means, this is a sophisticated measure that is difficult to employ unless unique circumstances exist. There are computer intercept control measures, referred to by the federal government as TEMPEST standards, that shield computers from both incoming and outgoing radio waves. This, however, is an expensive application that normally far exceeds the risk of a surveillance attack by this means.

EPILOGUE

. . . For the people resemble a wild beast, which, naturally fierce and accustomed to live in the woods, has been brought up, as it were, in a prison and in servitude, and having by accident got its liberty . . . easily becomes the prey of the first who seeks to incarcerate it again.

—Niccolo Machiavelli
Discourses on the First Ten Books of Titus Livius
Book II, Chapter 2

This book has introduced the reader to a unique and rarely documented perspective of personal security. The first chapter addressed the nature of the threat to personal privacy, and much of the text that followed addressed the various methods of intrusion and exploitation. As Machiavelli noted circa 1515, ignorance of the evil makes for an easy prey. The hunter will always conquer the hunted—unless the hunted becomes the hunter. The basis of survival is to avoid becoming the prey.

The world around us is a dangerous and hostile one. Whether spy versus spy, target versus terrorist, or you against the world, the keys to survival are the same. Although the enemy may not be readily apparent, accepting the fact that the enemy is everpresent is paramount to the preservation of personal security.

The underworld of crime and espionage is the battleground of shadow warriors who have survived in the face of the most sophisticated and hostile elements imaginable. Theirs is a highly predatory and often vicious world, of which the greater society is oblivious. These men without faces, and faces without names, will continue to fade anonymously into history and become lost in time like tears in the rain. It is truly unfortunate that their unrecorded episodes of intrigue and human confrontation will follow them into obscurity.

There is one legacy that remains for the benefit of those who will capitalize on the experiences of the shadow warriors. This book captures the principles and tactics of survival that they have developed, refined, and institutionalized throughout the years . . .

This book is dedicated to that legacy.